MEDIA AND THE AFFECTIVE LIFE OF SLAVERY

Media and the Affective Life of Slavery

Allison Page

University of Minnesota Press
Minneapolis
London

A different version of chapter 4 was previously published as "'How Many Slaves Work for You?' Race, New Media, and Neoliberal Consumer Activism," *Journal of Consumer Culture* 17, no. 1 (2017): 46–61. First published online October 8, 2014. Copyright 2017 SAGE. https://doi.org/10.1177/1469540514553716.

Published by the University of Minnesota Press
111 Third Avenue South, Suite 290
Minneapolis, MN 55401-2520
http://www.upress.umn.edu

ISBN 978-1-5179-1039-6 (hc)
ISBN 978-1-5179-1040-2 (pb)

A Cataloging-in-Publication record for this book is available
from the Library of Congress.

Printed on acid-free paper

The University of Minnesota is an equal-opportunity educator and employer.

UMP KEP

For Christopher, with love

Contents

Racial Formation and Post–Civil Rights Governance

In the U.S. race has always been dependent on the visual.
—Evelynn Hammonds, "New Technologies of Race"

In September 2013, the first episode of actor and comedian Azie Dungey's satirical web series *Ask a Slave* appeared on YouTube. Dressed in eighteenth-century garb—a pale yellow frock, white apron, and white bonnet—Dungey's character introduces herself as Lizzie Mae, "personal housemaid to President and Lady Washington," at the ready to field questions about slavery and life on the plantation from present-day (and predominantly white) tourists.[1] Drawn from her experiences as a historical reenactor at Mount Vernon, Dungey begins each episode with the disclaimer: "The following is based on real interactions I had while portraying a slave character at a popular historic site. Names have been changed to protect the guilty." In what has been called a "fun" way to learn history, *Ask a Slave* contests not just official remembrances of slavery but also how such memorialization both relies on and contributes to certain racial formations—in particular, white liberalism and an iteration of whiteness that is self-satisfied by its presumed colorblindness. Dungey dislocates historical reenactment from its typical (and often serious) context and transforms it into a comedic format available online for free. As Dungey explains in interviews, *Ask a Slave* is a satire "about race and our relationship to history, especially black history, as modern Americans. The point is not to convey facts, though it is based in fact. I may not give educational answers, but they are factual ones. . . . It's social commentary, not education, tho [*sic*] many seem to learn from it."[2] Across two seasons, some of the humor arises from the questions Lizzie Mae is asked (e.g., "Where do you send your children to school?" and "What do you do for fun?"); however, *Ask a Slave* produces a searing critique that extends beyond deriding obliviousness and ignorance. Through humor and emotion, especially disgust, Dungey challenges hegemonic histories and pedagogies of U.S. chattel slavery and troubles a teleological understanding of both history and time. Lizzie Mae's disgust, in particular, contests the often triumphant and whitewashed narrative typically portrayed at such reenactment sites.

A play with temporality is central to the series, particularly since Dungey's experiences as a reenactor brought to the fore the messiness of distinct temporal markers between *then* and *now* with respect to anti-Black racism. By drawing our attention to the ongoing legacy of slavery in the present day, Dungey troubles supposedly firm temporal boundaries. *Ask a Slave* thus offers a powerful counterdiscourse to the public history of historical reenactment sites by pillorying postrace arguments and narratives about slavery that ultimately bolster whiteness by evacuating race and racism. Through *Ask a Slave*'s blend of the eighteenth and twenty-first centuries, Dungey exposes how the racial formations of Blackness and whiteness continue to intertwine in the contemporary era; the production of whiteness through how it imagines Blackness is, moreover, reliant on a particular narrative of the history of chattel slavery that is haunted by what it chooses not to remember.[3] This includes the epistemologies and racial logics of slavery that are based on white fantasies of Blackness.

For example, during the first season's second episode, "Abolitioning," a white viewer asks Lizzie Mae if she has any white friends. She responds by introducing Mr. Tobias Lear, "my master's personal secretary and an abolitionist. . . . I always say, any abolitionist is a friend of mine." When Lizzie Mae asks Lear to share his views on slavery, he adamantly states that he "*detests* the institution of slavery." After a series of follow-up questions in which Lear reveals his liberal racism, an agitated Lizzie Mae takes a call from Marge Henschel of present-day Minnesota, who says that she agrees with Mr. Lear and thinks that slavery was "just horrible. Slave masters were awful, just terrible." Lear interrupts her: "Although the institution of slavery is morally reprehensible, there were, and are, some good slave masters and owners. For instance, Thomas Jefferson, for example."

Her face filled with disgust, Lizzie Mae replies, "Thomas Jefferson? He has sex with his slaves." Smiling, Lear raises his finger in agreement and says, "Aha, yes, indeed." Lizzie Mae is aghast and shakes her head in disbelief as Lear continues, "And there's old Bill down at Pohick Roll. Now, Old Bill gives his slaves bacon on Sundays. Who does not like bacon?" A defeated Lizzie Mae responds, "Well, I gotta say, I do enjoy bacon." Through Lear's positioning as a moral, ethical subject—a savior—who simultaneously defends slave owners and whiteness, Dungey exposes the figure of the white abolitionist as not outside the logics of chattel slavery. As such, Dungey offers a rejoinder to a celebratory narrative of white abolitionism as racial innocence. Lear is not in solidarity with actual Black people; rather, he constitutes himself through how he imagines Blackness, something Lizzie Mae stresses when she notes, "Mr. Lear, I'm starting to get the feeling that you've never actually talked to a Black person before." The series draws on this back-and-forth talk-show-like structure throughout, with Dungey using Lizzie Mae's facial expressions and nonverbal reactions to convey an emotional contestation to white liberal racism.

I begin *Media and the Affective Life of Slavery* with *Ask a Slave* to offer a recent example of how hegemonic media about the history of slavery has been challenged by Black feminist cultural production. *Media and the Affective Life of Slavery* interrogates the relationship between racial formation, affective governance, and media culture about U.S. chattel slavery while highlighting an interplay between dominant mediated constructions and their contestations. In particular, I focus on how U.S. media culture from the 1960s to the present plays an important and ongoing role in teaching viewers how to act and feel in accordance with new racial norms in an era defined by the supposed end of legal racism. Given the immense shifts of the postwar era with respect to race and racial formation, I contend that emotion, produced by the pedagogical use of the history of slavery, is a powerful site through which to shape and manage race and racialized subjectivity. *Media and the Affective Life of Slavery* explores how media and the visual—alongside policy, political discourse, consumer culture, and curricula—provide templates for racialized subjectivity through producing and disciplining emotion.

As part of this, *Media and the Affective Life of Slavery* theorizes the changes in racial formation within the broader era of "post–civil rights." The shift to official antiracism in the wake of World War II and the civil rights movement(s) required a modification in subject and racial formation, given that it became less acceptable to be openly racist. I suggest that residual, dominant, and emergent formations complicate this periodization, revealing whiteness's adaptive maneuvers to contain antiracist activism threatening the dominance of white supremacy. Critically, media play a key role in teaching viewers and users about new racial norms, behaviors, and feelings that align with racial upheavals in the post-1960s era. *Media and the Affective Life of Slavery* examines media culture's role in these processes, theorizing media as not just a system of representation but also as an affective technology of citizenship and subjectivity where race is constructed as a problem to be solved using visual mediums. I draw on archival research to consider the role of news and entertainment television, curricula, video games, and digital apps in educating the U.S. public about slavery in order to produce and navigate post–civil rights racial formations. Constructing and using the history of slavery, these media instruct viewers in how to behave and feel in line with the particular sociohistorical moments in which they are situated; such emphasis on emotion frequently works to obscure structural concerns like racialized disparities in health, incarceration, housing, and wealth.

Media pedagogy about slavery and race is therefore central to racialized subject formation, as viewers are guided in how to feel and understand themselves in racialized terms. There has been a recent upturn in media depictions of U.S. chattel slavery, including more than seven films released in 2013 alone and the History Channel's updated version of *Roots,* released in May 2016. Mainstream movies like *Antebellum* (2020), *Harriet* (2019), *Free State of Jones* (2016), *The Birth of a Nation* (2016), and *Freedom* (2014) continue this resurgence. This media interest has accompanied broader debates about slavery's relation to contemporary racial disparities in poverty, incarceration, housing, and education.[4] *Media and the Affective Life of Slavery* historicizes periodic cultural fixations on the history of U.S. chattel slavery as imagined by and through media culture to address the questions guiding my project, including: What is the relationship between a pedagogical impetus to educate on a broad scale about the history of U.S. chattel slavery and the state's turn to official antiracism? What is the role of affective governance—particularly through media culture—in relation to race and racial formation? How do emotions help to constitute race and racialized subjectivity? Although there has been a relative abundance of U.S. media content about the history of Atlantic slavery in the period I am examining, I have chosen to focus on my objects in part because of their formal relation to an era's predominant racial formation, a point that I elaborate on below.

The Visual and Slavery's Afterlives

Despite significant moments when media produce programming on slavery, critical media studies has rarely taken up the question of slavery's depiction and, further, the uses to which depictions have been put. This oversight in the discipline's literature holds despite the fact that television, film, photography, living history museums, postage stamps, and plantation tourism are key cultural and pedagogical sites where slavery is popularly represented. Critical scholarship on representations of slavery comes primarily from literary studies and Black studies and often focuses on novels, slave narratives, and visual culture.[5] Because media culture dominates our current moment and popular media are key sites for the production of meaning about slavery, this absence within critical media studies is significant. As I underscore in *Media and the Affective Life of Slavery*, how we view race is inextricable from the history of slavery, which is foundational to the visual—including popular media—and to ways of seeing. Moreover, as scholars like Saidiya Hartman, Christina Sharpe, Michelle Commander, Kimberly Juanita Brown, and Alys Weinbaum observe, part of how the current moment is shaped by slavery is epistemic.[6] Hartman's theorization of the "afterlife of slavery," which refers to the incalculable ways that slavery still lives on in the present, derives from a "racial calculus" instilled centuries ago that produces and devalues Blackness and Black life. Hartman points to skewed life chances, health inequities, impoverishment, and the continued criminalization of Blackness as evidence of slavery's afterlife and reach into the present. As such, the afterlife of slavery is a conception of history and time that is not progressive but rather considers how slavery's residue persists in shaping life and death in the United States.[7] Slavery's afterlife endures in innumerable ways, including the racial logics that have shapeshifted to adapt to a different era yet continue to underpin formations like liberalism and capitalism. *Media and the Affective of Slavery* is in conversation with this body of work to consider how the epistemological remains of U.S. chattel slavery inform media culture beyond the politics of representation.

Along these lines, *Media and the Affective Life of Slavery* demonstrates the centrality of mediated engagements with slavery to post–civil rights racial formation, which I suggest is inextricable from affective governance. *Affective governance* refers to the production and management of affect and emotion to align with governing rationalities; in *Media and the Affective Life of Slavery*, I trace the shift to official antiracism and neoliberal governmentality and argue that changing racial formations—entangled with capital's movements—require the cultivation of particular emotions. I use *affect* and *emotion* here in the sense articulated by Sara Ahmed in *The Cultural Politics of Emotion*, wherein she notes that she does not separate "sensation or affect and emotion" in the manner of Brian Massumi, for whom affect is sensation prior to discourse.[8] Massumi's theorization of affect as bodily intensity that is presocial and prelinguistic differs from Ahmed's theorization in that Ahmed understands bodily sensations to be bound up with—not distinct from—emotion. Moreover, Ahmed does not see strong boundaries between emotion and affect but rather understands them as deeply intertwined. Likewise, I use *affect* and *emotion* interchangeably.

My concern is with the political and collective possibilities of emotion, as well as their molding in the service of maintaining the status quo. In this way, I focus on media's role in shaping and governing racialized populations through the cultivation and management of emotion, and the interconnectedness of racial formation to this process. For example, television documentaries during the 1960s worked to contain and temper antiracist activism, shoring up the ideal subject as rational, disinterested, and without individual prejudice. By contrast, the curricula based on the 1977 television miniseries *Roots* instructed white viewers to feel admiration and sympathy for African Americans, whereas Black viewers were taught a particular kind of pride, one unthreatening to white supremacy and racial capitalism. The curricular emphasis on emotion constituted a form of affective governance that occluded larger structural concerns of the era, including an increasing racialized wealth gap, the concentrated effort to undo the gains of the civil rights movement(s), and the implementation of neoliberal policies that left deindustrialized cities in ruin.

As I show throughout *Media and the Affective Life of Slavery*, certain media about slavery generate particular feelings and emotional states that work to turn the racial "problems" of a specific historical moment into a safe racial orientation. This aligns with shifting racial formations and contributes to them; importantly, these different formations are also connected to media forms. As an example, during the 1960s, television documentaries were predominant in a way that they are not today. The objects I focus on are chosen for this reason—for instance, chapter 3's educational video game about slavery, *Flight to Freedom*, points to an emergent entanglement of the production of race through code and algorithmic media. Although I do not focus heavily on formal analysis, the form of each chapter's media is significant in that the effectiveness of the pedagogy around race and emotion is tied to it. A documentary about the history of U.S. chattel slavery today, for example, would not have the same pedagogical import as the video game or chapter 4's website and app, Slavery Footprint. Media contribute to racial formation, certainly, but this extends beyond content and the politics of representation. As I argue throughout *Media and the Affective Life of Slavery*, media are also biopolitical, capable of discipline and management at the level of population through both the affordances of form and their broader uptake in concert with policy, political discourse, and institutions. Moreover, the objects I examine are pedagogical; this is why, for instance, I examine the educational video game *Flight to Freedom* rather than commercial games like *Assassin's Creed*. By attending to the media environment as well as how racial formation operates, I suggest that certain media are more pedagogically effective for governing rationalities in a particular era. This is pertinent given that the objects I examine are also constituted as progressive texts.[9]

Despite the distance that hegemonic media culture attempts to create between the antebellum era and the contemporary one, slavery continues to haunt the present—a haunting that is made visible by media, even if inadvertently. Although the texts I examine are primarily white-produced prescriptive ones, I suggest that there is unintended excess—what Avery Gordon calls a "seething presence"—that cannot be understood or theorized solely by a governmentality analytic.[10] Thus, mediated engagements with the history of slavery reveal complex interactions with temporality, capital, pedagogy, and racial formation. Because we need to attend to these, we cannot restrict our attention to governing rationalities alone. As such, we must think through affect, visuality, and haunting alongside thinking through the analytics of governance and race. These "restless ghosts" that haunt mark a significant threat to the United States in that, as Lisa Marie Cacho writes, "the dead can force us all to reckon with the violences that produced them."[11] The texts I examine in *Media and the Affective Life of Slavery* are haunted by the possibility of revealing the violence foundational to the United States; as a threat to the status quo, this is managed through an emphasis on progress narratives and certain "safe" emotions, like admiration. Such emotions are crucial to racial formation, particularly the constitution of white racial innocence and what Robin DiAngelo terms "white fragility."[12]

The "occult presence" of slavery's haunting grip on the present is, for David Marriott, a presence that is "nowhere but nevertheless everywhere, a dead time which never arrives and does not stop arriving, as though by arriving it never happened until it happens again, then it never happened."[13] Rather than a telos, time is unending. The question of temporality arises in *Media and the Affective Life of Slavery* most starkly in relation to the hegemonic progress narrative that dominates discourses of racial struggle in the United States. This teleological view of history and time relies on the history of slavery as a starting point to mark racial progress. It is thereby a distancing maneuver, one that locates slavery firmly in the past. Acknowledging the legacies of slavery becomes a way to overcome them, which shifts blame for the afterlife of slavery to Black pathology. This, in turn, allows whiteness—in crisis during the civil rights and Black Power era—to reconsolidate as nonculpable; the state's official antiracism required white people to similarly perform outward antiracism, in part through the appropriate expression and management of emotion in relation to race. As I demonstrate, this is inextricable from the visual, with spectators divided along a Black/white racial line continuing to see differently even as the history of racial trauma and oppression is ongoing and visible.[14] The visual has the capacity to remind us of what Alexander Weheliye suggests "covertly underpins modern political formations, namely visual instantiations of naked life or the hieroglyphics of flesh."[15] Black feminist theorists and critical scholars of slavery draw our attention to how this is a gendered formation, bound up with the subjugation of Black women.[16] Azie Dungey's *Ask a Slave* offers a mediated instance of a Black feminist theorization of the circularity of time that underscores the sexual violence central to slavery, rendered visible through Lizzie Mae's disgusted reaction to particular questions. When a white man asks in a lascivious manner, "Hey, Lizzie Mae, show me where you're branded," Lizzie Mae responds by flipping him off.[17] Just as Dungey complicates the figure of the white abolitionist, so too does she take on the triumphant discourse about Thomas Jefferson as heroic and, at worst, as merely a man of his time. When asked about the worst day of her life, Lizzie Mae replies, "The day Thomas Jefferson came over. Next question."[18]

The Post–Civil Rights Era and Entangled Racial Formation

Media and the Affective Life of Slavery centers objects from the 1960s and beyond in order to trace media culture's role in shifting racial formations and state power wrought by the activism of the 1960s and 1970s. In particular, I emphasize the move to "official antiracism," which altered post–World War II racial formation and citizenship when the state began positioning itself as antiracist. This change occurred in part due to Cold War anxieties about combating the paradox of racial inequality at home and espousing anti–Soviet Union rhetoric that positioned the United States as open and free in contrast to a closed and communist form of governance.[19] Rather than a progress narrative in which racial justice activists and advocates confront ongoing modifications to white supremacy after the "racial break" of the postwar era, the notion of official antiracism allows us to see how the state and capital guided both the incorporation of and capitalization on minority difference.[20]

Whereas the concept of a racial break reproduces a teleological sense of time, with racial justice and white supremacy in a dialectical struggle unfolding in a forward-moving direction, Jodi Melamed's theorization of official antiracism during this era underscores the circularity of time and the capacity of white supremacy to engender new violence—epistemic and otherwise—through what appears to be formally antiracist discourse. Against a progress narrative, official antiracism identifies how the state, capital, and U.S. university structured postwar U.S. racial formation by incorporating antiracist discourse and knowledges in ways that perpetuate white supremacy in a new era. In other words, the act of incorporation itself is a continuation of racism, not its amelioration.

Capital is central to and profits from this maneuver. By severing race from material conditions, the official antiracism put forth by the state and other realms makes it possible to seem antiracist while furthering the very systems reliant on white supremacy, like racial capitalism. The dematerialization of antiracist discourse enables the negation of social movement efforts (particularly those of formations like women of color feminism) and legitimizes grossly asymmetrical material conditions, all while appearing antiracist.[21] The changes in racial formation within the post–civil rights period are thus attendant on the shift from liberalism and a Keynesian welfare state to the beginnings of neoliberalism in the 1970s.[22] As a governing rationality, economic philosophy, and racial project, neoliberalism operates in tandem with emergent formations—for instance, a budding multiculturalism, apparent in the Ethnic Heritage Studies Act of 1974. The passage of this act resulted in funds for educational programs and curricula to discover one's ethnic heritage; simultaneously, this genealogical interest in finding one's roots and the affective instruction of the *Roots* miniseries occluded from view the neoliberal restructuring taking place at this moment, including widespread deindustrialization, deregulation, and privatization. In the supposedly postrace Obama era, the website and digital app Slavery Footprint's attempt to render race into information and data is a move indebted to neoliberal understandings of race as no longer relevant.

Media and the Affective Life of Slavery is concerned with how media grapple with the history of slavery in light of the state's positioning as antiracist and the role of affective governance in this process. Given the immense social, economic, and political changes of the postwar era, the category "whiteness" underwent large fluctuations. With the activism of the civil rights and Black Power movements, whiteness was thrown into crisis and began to reconsolidate in the wake of challenges to its dominance yet could not do so on the same terms as before. Overt white supremacy was no longer socially acceptable in the ways it once was; whiteness needed to rebuild itself anew and recast its supremacy, in part through characterizing whiteness as antiracist.[23] In chapter 1, I detail this moment of whiteness in crisis and consider the affective dispositions encouraged by media culture as a resolution. I argue that media play a crucial role in constituting and perpetuating official antiracism through the pedagogical deployment of the history of U.S. chattel slavery to shape and manage emotion. My chapters thus explore how emotions—produced by mediated engagement with the history of U.S. chattel slavery—are shaped and guided to bolster changing racial formations, demonstrating the centrality of affective governance to race and racialized subjectivity. The texts I examine are widely understood to be progressive in nature, without explicitly conservative aims; their pedagogical and disciplinary address is refracted through a lens of antiracism aimed at producing liberal (and later, neoliberal) citizen-subjects who understand themselves as antiracist even as racial disparities intensify in housing, education, and incarceration.

The relationality of whiteness and Blackness as intertwined racial formations is essential to *Media and the Affective Life of Slavery*. This relationship is particularly evident during the antebellum era, disrupting the misconception that slavery is only about Blackness and anti-Blackness. It is that, certainly, but it was also about the production of whiteness—enslaved Black people were the vehicles through which white people came to know themselves and to materialize their aspirations.[24] The entangling of Blackness and whiteness is likewise not separate from the production of emotion: for example, as I demonstrate in chapter 1, 1960s television documentaries establish Blackness as irrational, angry, and excessive, thereby marking whiteness as rational, objective, and justified. In her work on the biopolitics of emotion, Kyla Schuller points to how white feelings—"fertile products"—are constituted precisely through their relation to "racialized vulnerability, disposability, and death."[25] Emotion is part of white racial formation, but this extends beyond racialized fears about Blackness to include the feelings of antiracism. Feeling antiracist can look like liberal multiculturalism and appreciating difference, but it can also look like pity, sympathy, and guilt.

Beyond Representational Politics

One of the tensions present throughout *Media and the Affective Life of Slavery* is between emotion and the supposed neutrality of data as means to address race and racism. To theorize this relationship, I rely on a conceptual framework that combines governmentality with critical theories of race and affect in order to attend to that which falls outside of the category "rational." In this way, *Media and the Affective Life of Slavery* understands media culture in a biopolitical rather than solely representational sense.[26] A biopolitical understanding of media culture considers how media operate as (and collaborate with) cultural technologies that work to shape and manage populations. Although slavery has not been a specific concern for most media studies scholars, questions of race have been examined within media studies for decades, and the politics of representation, in particular, has preoccupied scholars working to address denigrating and racist imagery. *Media and the Affective Life of Slavery* is in conversation with this crucial scholarship, while also focusing on media as a cultural technology—complicit with technologies of governance like prisons and schools—rather than only or primarily as a site of identity formation and representation. Shaping and managing both race and emotion are key components of governance; I explore the intersection between the two as they relate to governance.

Considering governmentality, in addition to representation, draws our attention toward the hierarchies of value that undergird the notion of so-called positive images and the search for good role models, families, and bodies. Demonstrating how citizens and subjects are produced for particular social, political, and economic rationalities, governmentality has been fruitful in that it considers how a text is used within political rationalities toward certain ends.[27] For example, Anna McCarthy shows how 1950s state and nonstate groups, including corporations and sponsors, sought to use early television as a technology for producing and managing citizens during the Cold War era.[28] A governmentality analytic is thus concerned with the pedagogical aims and purposes of a text rather than whether it is stereotypical or not, or whether ideology is working or not.[29] In a moment where there has been a "proliferation of difference" in media culture, this analytic moves us away from a primary focus on the politics of representation.[30] Governmentality can capture more of why, for instance, *Roots* was aired in 1977 in the wake of the civil rights and Black Power movements rather than solely attending to how the miniseries represented its characters.[31]

Within media and cultural studies, governmentality has been used to make sense of various cultural phenomena, including the rise of self-help culture, reality television, surveillance, and ethical consumption.[32] In particular, the work of Laurie Ouellette and James Hay has been foundational for exploring how media enact strategies of governance—especially the transformation of individuals and populations into "active, responsible citizens"—through the circulation of pedagogical resources for everyday self-management and self-transformation.[33] Although this scholarship is especially helpful for understanding how reality television operates as a governing technology, it does not consider the relationship between race and governmentality. "Techniques of subjectification" function to transform individuals in ways that align with norms, including those of behavior, health, and affect; race is central to this process.[34] The objects I examine work alongside and within political discourse to guide viewers toward norms of thought, behavior, and affect with respect to changing racial formations and the shift to neoliberal governmentality.

Given governmentality's focus on subject formation and liberal citizenship, and Foucauldian conceptions of power as productive, *Media and the Affective Life of Slavery* considers how the state's embrace of minority difference required accompanying affective states, including a feeling of antiracism. The passage of the Ethnic Heritage Studies Act during 1972 (funded in 1974), for instance, worked to include minoritized subjects and certain histories within a progress narrative of the nation. This was accompanied by a discourse of multiculturalism evident in the curricula developed with funds from the act. As a 1977 *New York Times* article notes, although the "roots movement" to discover one's ethnic heritage was bolstered by the passage of the act, the *Roots* miniseries itself is largely responsible for increasing genealogical interest: "John La Corte, founder and director of the

Genealogical Heraldic Institute of America, says that inquiries have more than doubled since the broadcasts."[35] Significantly, most of the act's funds were directed to universities.

In chapter 1, I argue that shifting racial formations in the postwar era were bound up with the production and disciplining of emotion—particularly rage and fear—as evidenced in the spate of television documentaries on race, slavery, and civil rights that aired during the decade. Alongside the golden age of television documentary in the mid-twentieth century, television news coverage began establishing itself in relation to the racial violence and terror made visible by antiracist action. The civil rights movement and the relatively young medium desperate to be taken seriously engendered an unlikely alliance between activists and industry. For the civil rights movement, sympathetic news coverage of the atrocities endured by activists and others was a strategic and conscious tactic, with the civil rights movement becoming the "first major domestic story, or theme, for television news in particular."[36] For an industry seeking to recover its legitimacy in the wake of the quiz show scandals of the 1950s, in which it was revealed that immensely popular TV quiz shows were actually rigged in advance, the civil rights movement offered a means toward gravitas.[37] Critically, the industry's desire for national expansion and legitimacy depended on images of white terrorism against Black Americans; in this way, Black visual trauma is central to the origins of television and television news. In 1964, CBS president Frank Stanton addressed the National Broadcast Editorial Conference of the Columbia University Graduate School of Journalism, calling for "commitment and advocacy" in the wake of Lyndon B. Johnson's signing of the Voting Rights Act of 1964. Describing the moment as a "pivotal point in our history," Stanton urged broadcasters "to use their 5,000 voices heard on 156 million radio sets and 61 million television sets, in a mighty continuing editorial crusade to make this new law work."[38]

Chapter 1 draws on four 1960s television documentaries to suggest that they contributed to the pathologization of Black anger, which in turn produced white innocence and fear. The documentary form, infused with authority, rationality, and emotional detachment, provided a container for emotions constituted as excessive and threatening in an era of rupture. Emotion is critical here, with the

documentaries functioning as a guide to Black anger for white viewers mystified by the era's turmoil, while also producing and intensifying white fears of Black revolutionary violence and struggle. As
the chapter suggests, by teaching lessons about slavery and race, the
documentaries contributed to the production of official antiracism
and made the regulation of emotion a central part of the process.
By the 1970s, the tension between a statistical and detached approach to racism and an emotional one attentive to changing one's
feelings tilted toward the latter. Chapter 2 argues that it became
important in this decade to feel in ways that aligned with broader
changes taking place in terms of the state's shift to official antiracism
and the attendant fluctuations in the production of whiteness and
Blackness. The enthusiasm for an emotional response to racism and
the history of U.S. chattel slavery is made especially plain in the discourse surrounding the 1977 television miniseries *Roots,* which told
the story of a family enduring American slavery over the span of two
hundred years. I argue that the series and its broader cultural uptake
attempted to incorporate African Americans as part of the nation
and to teach the proper feelings with respect to slavery and race for
a new era and racial order: whereas the television documentaries
sought to manage escalating Black insurrection through objectivity
and distance, in this instance, television teaches viewers how to feel
about U.S. chattel slavery and its ongoing legacies. White viewers are
instructed to feel admiration and sympathy for African Americans,
while Black viewers are taught to feel pride in a past recuperated
through the hero, Kunta Kinte. Documentary offered an authoritative and putatively unbiased way to deal with the history of slavery
logically rather than through emotion—Black anger, in particular,
was a threat the documentaries sought to contain through detached
explanation. By contrast, the melodramatic form of *Roots* is key to
sentimental education in that melodrama encourages a cathartic
experience where viewers feel and then resolve those feelings, leading to closure. Sentimental education thus works to engender certain feelings that help facilitate the cultural shift from the immediate
post–civil rights era to multiculturalism and colorblindness. The
Roots emphasis on feeling in turn occludes from view structural racism and the racialized flow of wealth in the United States, especially
pertinent during the 1970s in the face of neoliberal restructuring like

deindustrialization that left cities and communities in ruin. Simultaneously, learning and adopting particular feelings and emotional states with respect to issues of slavery, race, and racism contributed to the reshaping of whiteness during the 1970s.

Chapter 3 assesses the shift to neoliberal multiculturalism and traces the requisite emotions undergirding this formation, particularly empathy and agency. To do so, I examine the educational role-playing video game *Flight to Freedom,* designed to teach middle school students about the history of slavery in the United States. In *Flight to Freedom,* the second game in the *Mission U.S.* series, players inhabit the character Lucy, a fourteen-year-old girl enslaved in 1848, two years before the passage of the Fugitive Slave Act. Set in northern Kentucky and southern Ohio, the game begins with Lucy on the King plantation outside Lexington. Divided into five parts plus prologue and epilogue, the game requires students to navigate choices provided in order to help Lucy "find a path to freedom." *Flight to Freedom* is part of a larger curriculum with an interactive website featuring teacher's guides, activities, and primary source documents that, promotional materials claim, "show the broader social, political, and economic context of events and perspectives featured in the game."[39] I contend that the racialized relationship of empathy for the slave through immersion—according to the game's discourse, one "becomes" a slave through playing the game—is central to racialized governance and a shift to an imagined postracial future, wherein whiteness is constituted in part through empathizing with a racialized other. The game works as a technology of citizenship and the self, offering civic instruction and emphasizing the importance of agency to garner respect and diversify access to the category "human." In the game, the Black body is not passive or wounded; rather, it is agential. Although the game is aimed at all students, *Flight to Freedom* and *Mission U.S.* are part of a larger effort by PBS-supported educational groups to manage "risky" populations—namely, young students of color at risk of "dropping out" of school. The game's emphasis on rehabilitating Blackness by constituting enslaved people as agents is a (neo)liberal maneuver, one that relies on particular notions of personhood and citizenship; as such, I place *Flight to Freedom* in a longer genealogy of public media's civic function.

The final chapter considers the entanglement of race, emotion, algorithmic governance, and digital media in the shift toward an emergent formation presuming the neutrality of data. I investigate the website Slavery Footprint and accompanying digital app—a collaboration between a nonprofit organization (Made in a Free World) and the U.S. State Department—which purport to measure an individual's "slavery footprint." I examine Slavery Footprint as part of the broader shift toward algorithmic management of emotion in relation to race. Much like *Flight to Freedom,* Slavery Footprint uses interactivity as a means toward racial understanding, though Slavery Footprint bypasses any acknowledgment of race altogether in lieu of a transnational and colorblind notion of difference, one where U.S. consumers function as saviors of a racialized other. This is underscored in the site's pedagogical use of the history of U.S. chattel slavery, which is deployed to add moral heft and urgency to address what it calls modern-day or twenty-first-century slavery. In so doing, Slavery Footprint and Made in a Free World locate slavery elsewhere both temporally and spatially, and therefore erase the afterlife of slavery and the salience of anti-Black racism to everyday life. Through a reliance on algorithms and data to uncover what they term slavery, Made in a Free World promulgates the notion of the digital not only as neutral and separate from race and capitalism but also as a prime solution. Within a context of neoliberal poverty management and consumer activism, Slavery Footprint produces a form of ethical subjectivity that thinks about, and acts against, race and racism through consumption and digital media rather than emotion.

Scholars and writers like Toni Morrison, Toni Cade Bambara, and Margaret Walker were retheorizing and reimagining the history of U.S. chattel slavery through a Black feminist lens at the same time that *Roots* became a focal point for issues of race and the legacies of slavery in the United States.[40] In the conclusion, I return to the frame that I began with at this introduction: namely, how Black feminist cultural production has theorized, countered, and challenged dominant uses of the history of slavery to shape emotion and subjectivity. I examine the video piece, *An Audience,* that artist Kara Walker created to address how audiences engaged with her giant sugar sphinx, *A Subtlety.* I suggest that Walker demonstrates that the violence of this history and its reach into the present is complex and layered in ways that are not reducible to innocence or feeling the supposedly correct

feelings. Like Azie Dungey, Walker's work offers a vision of history
and time as circular rather than linear; in so doing, both Dungey and
Walker challenge whiteness and white liberalism, certainly, but also
emphasize its slipperiness and persistence, in part through the racialization of emotions. Dungey, for example, underscores the phenomenon of "white women's tears" in the episode "New Leaf, Same
Page," during which a white woman named Colleen tears up after
Lizzie Mae explains how much sewing she must do on her "down
time": "Oh my God, that is just so . . . I can't imagine how anyone
with a conscience would actually, like, make people be enslaved."[41]
Lizzie Mae responds by asking Colleen if she knows her seamstress
and when Colleen says she does not, Lizzie Mae replies, "Then how
do you know she ain't in the same position I am?" Dungey thus
critiques individual claims of antiracist sentiment with a lack of attention to larger structural issues, such as contemporary racialized
and gendered labor practices, and showcases how white liberalism
is quick to condemn slavery while simultaneously participating in
its ongoing racial logics. Overall, the conclusion demonstrates the
ongoing Black feminist contestation—through visual cultural production, in particular—of chattel slavery's residue and effects in the
contemporary era.

"The Restless Black Peril"

Race, Television Documentary, and Emotion

*We started out wondering what, if anything, in this country
reflects the fact that there had been slavery here. . . . What we
found was that old relationships still persist in many subtle
and some blatant ways.*

—Peter Davis, producer, "The Heritage of Slavery"

I n a 1968 *Los Angeles Times* article promoting the seven-episode
television documentary series *Of Black America*, white executive
producer Perry Wolff revealed his understanding of the inheritances
of U.S. chattel slavery: "The Negroes aren't slaves anymore but they
suffer a form of psychological slavery. . . . Many of them still have the
feeling whites do it all better and they feel there's white superiority
although they won't say it. The Negro must get rid of his psychological chains."[1] Such pathologization of the Black psyche was certainly
not new—the long history of a racialized metric of mental "fitness"
for citizenship being but one example—yet during the 1960s, when
activists were fervently contesting the existing racial order and its
attendant hierarchy of value, the pathologizing took on a new va-
lence. For Wolff, the supposedly injured Black psyche was evidence
of slavery's residue in the present. Echoing the therapeutic ethos of
the era, Wolff places the onus on Black people to liberate themselves
psychologically as the means to ending the ongoing legacy of slavery.
Such "psychological chains" in this theorization are attached to emotion, to residual feelings of inadequacy that, according to Wolff, keep
Black people in "chains." The imperative "must" erases white supremacy and promulgates a notion of racism as simply a state of mind. The

required response, then, is merely to reshape one's thoughts and feelings, a burden that Wolff places on African Americans.

Wolff was not alone in suggesting emotional management as a solution to the era's turmoil. In this chapter, I argue that shifting racial formations in the postwar era were bound up with the production and disciplining of emotion—particularly rage and fear—as evidenced in the spate of television documentaries on race, slavery, and civil rights that aired during the decade. Drawing on the *Bell & Howell Close-Up!* episode "Cast the First Stone" (1960), the *CBS Reports* episodes "The Harlem Temper" (1963) and "Black Power, White Backlash" (1966), and *Of Black America*'s "The Heritage of Slavery" (1968), I suggest that the documentaries contributed to the pathologization of Black anger in ways that reinforced white innocence and fear. Critically, the form of the documentary, which has been infused with authority, rationality, and emotional detachment, works here as a receptacle for emotions constructed as excessive and threatening, a particularly salient containment during an era of upheaval. The long-standing entanglement of Black and white racial formations, where whiteness understands and produces itself through how it imagines Blackness, occurs in part through the governance of emotion.[2]

Despite the fact that many of the documentaries featured a range of Black participants, including Black nationalists, they were geared toward white audiences and framed their content accordingly.[3] Not in the least about Black empowerment, the documentaries sought to educate white viewers about the past as a means of tempering the present and preventing further erosion of white life. The documentaries thus connected contemporary racial strife—constituted as an issue divided solely along a Black/white color line—to slavery. Emotion is central here, with the documentaries operating as a guide to Black anger for white viewers perplexed by the era's uprisings, while simultaneously producing and bolstering white fears of Black revolutionary violence and struggle. By teaching lessons about slavery—and, by extension, race—the documentaries contributed to the production of official antiracism and made the disciplining of emotion key to this process. The temporal contradictions of the programs, with slavery relegated to the past but also acknowledged as affecting the present, enabled whiteness to reconstitute as nonculpable for contemporary racism and inequality. While steeped in an allure of progressivism, the programs examined here worked to quell Black resistance by securing white concessions, constituting whiteness as antiracist and rational, and bolstering white fear of Black radical struggle. The construction of whiteness as antiracist, moreover, relied on a burgeoning discourse about Black pathology. Pathologizing Black people and Blackness, television documentaries in turn constructed whiteness as innocent and blameless.

Whiteness in Crisis

The production of race through the disciplining and governance of emotion was not a new phenomenon, certainly, but it took on a different urgency and character during the 1960s.[4] As a "discourse of sobriety," the documentary form lent its seriousness to addressing and managing the racial volatility of the United States at midcentury.[5] From civil rights activism in the earlier part of the decade, to the 1965 Watts Rebellion in Los Angeles, to the rise of Black Power and the student movements, the 1960s were years of intense struggle around white supremacy, racial capitalism, and legalized apartheid. The inner city and student uprisings of the 1960s contested ongoing anti-Black violence, including police brutality and the assassinations of both Martin Luther King Jr. and Malcolm X, and were animated by anger at the poverty "left untouched by civil rights legislation."[6] To address what was constituted as the "problem" of Black responses to institutional violence and the crisis of whiteness, the documentaries urged viewers to reflect on slavery and racism in rational, controlled ways; the work of television documentary in this era was understood as promoting rational thought to combat the feminized emotion of television's "vast wasteland."[7] Writing in 1965, scholar A. William Bluem describes the purpose of documentary: "If we add the responsibilities of journalism to documentary, we realize that only by undistorted appraisal of the crises in American life can rational men report the facts as they see them. They may introduce the scenes of anger and hate, but they must also help us to maintain detachment."[8] Led by "rational men," television documentary intervened in an otherwise dangerous field of emotion and provided a blueprint for its management.[9]

Furthermore, addressing slavery through the documentary form

was a means to put the continued legacy of slavery to rest. The contradictions of the documentaries center on this paradox: how to acknowledge the impact of slavery while highlighting national progress.
By presenting the nation as antiracist, free, and concerned with democracy and equality, the documentaries gesture toward the effects
of slavery lingering in the present in ways that locate slavery in the
past. In so doing, the issue of Black poverty—a result of slavery—is
renarrated by the temporal contradiction as Black pathology. Pathology thus becomes an explanation given that slavery is located in the
past (soon to be joined by white racism), and the white audience of
the documentaries is provided a way to come to terms with slavery
without hindering their present. Instead, the vestiges of slavery are
borne by Black people; white people are thereby let off the hook.

Yet the documentaries were not alone in promulgating slavery
as an explanation for what was pathologized as a "culture of poverty," wherein the poor are considered to be flawed reproducers of a
failed way of life that results in ongoing insecurity.[10] The documentaries were part of an emergent white liberalism that used the devastations of slavery to explain "black pathology," as exemplified by the
Moynihan Report. Published by Daniel Patrick Moynihan in 1965 as
The Negro Family: The Case for National Action, the report argued that
widening gaps between Black and white Americans in areas including
education, income, and access to health care should be attributed to
a broken and "unstable family structure" within Black communities.
According to Moynihan, this "crumbling" family structure (which
for him meant the dissolution of heteronormativity) was the result
of slavery and was evidenced by single mothers and "disintegrating
Negro marriage," yielding welfare dependency. For Moynihan, "The
Negro was given liberty but not equality. . . . Keeping the Negro 'in
his place' can be translated as keeping the Negro male in his place:
the female was not a threat to anyone. Unquestionably, these events
worked against the emergence of a strong father figure."[11] As a liberal
maneuver, the Moynihan Report acknowledged slavery's devastations only as a means of pathologizing, disciplining, and managing
Black communities, particularly Black mothers.

Such use of "damage imagery" has a long history within social science and, as Moynihan himself exemplifies, is not limited to conser-

vatives; liberal experts similarly produced and relied on "images of blacks as damaged . . . specifically to aid the cause of obtaining black rights and opportunities."[12] Moynihan drew upon Stanley Elkins's *Slavery*, which suggested that "the black male, as an extension of his master's will, was docile and thus controllable."[13] Despite their ostensibly progressive intent, liberals ultimately worked against eliminating white supremacy, relying on a presumption that white Americans would support Black freedom and equality only if Black people "were made to appear psychologically damaged and granted a special status as victims."[14] This, in effect, bolstered the hierarchy of value and racial order undergirding white supremacy, enabling white people to feel superior and whole by contrast. Whiteness relies on a degraded Blackness—this enables us to see that although chattel slavery was about Blackness and anti-Blackness, it was also about the production of whiteness.

The postwar era's budding white liberalism was part of a broader set of shifts occurring in relation to whiteness and racial formation. The transformations taking place within the United States and globally—including new conceptions of race post–World War II, the Cold War, changes in immigration law, emergent forms of post-Fordist capitalism, and international decolonization struggles—contributed to the postwar era's status as a time of immense change, particularly as global activism caused ruptures that forced white supremacy and whiteness into crisis.[15] Attendant sociopolitical struggles, including the politicization of "the historical violences of white supremacy" wrought by World War II, produced a reckoning that Jodi Melamed suggests made visible the connections between "European fascism, racial segregation, and colonial rule."[16] As such, returning war veterans began to see internal racial apartheid in the United States as an issue inseparable from decolonization efforts abroad.

Because race was considered the unifying concern during this era of crisis, resolutions were centered on race, giving rise to a "formally antiracist, liberal-capitalist modernity determined by and shaping the conditions of U.S. global ascendancy."[17] This new logic thus sprang from the U.S. nation-state's attempts to quell militancy and civil unrest, becoming a "mode of discipline for all minoritized subjects" even as it also seduced and appealed as a mode of inclusion.[18]

Formal antiracism required the reshaping of institutions, including U.S. higher education, as part of the hegemonic affirmation of minority difference in the wake of widespread disruptions of the status quo. Rather than considered simply an interruption for hegemony, minority difference was used in its service as well, resulting in the production of new epistemologies and discourses about race and difference.

At the same time, whiteness as a racial formation was adapting to this era in which overt white supremacy was no longer socially acceptable. Brought to crisis by civil rights activism and Black resistance, whiteness could not reconsolidate on the same terms as before and thus sought to rebuild and recast its supremacy to "accord with the language of equal rights"—in other words, to reconstitute as antiracist.[19] Conceding some became a way to avoid conceding a lot, and according to Steve Martinot, this begrudging "ethical progress made by white society" could at base be theorized as "a pragmatic mode of crisis management" in response to "black rage at white reticence to obey its own laws and ideals."[20] The documentaries were part of the production and management of racialized emotion, where the constitution of Blackness as angry and excessively emotional produced whiteness as detached and rational.

For instance, during the 1966 *CBS Reports* episode "Black Power, White Backlash," narrator Mike Wallace interviews several Black activists, but rather than engage their points about white supremacy and ongoing discrimination, he repeatedly turns the conversation to violence, depicting the activists as focused on violence for violence's sake and erasing the concerns undergirding their struggle. With a condescending tone reserved for Black interviewees, Wallace portrays militant Black activism as unjustifiably angry and irrational, even going so far as to bring in a statistician at the end of the program to underscore the erosion of white sympathy for Black civil rights, a loss attributed to violence. The takeaway message is that if Black people had not "rioted" during the summer of 1966, they would still have white support, a gift to be bestowed on those deemed deserving of it. This monologue presents whiteness as calm, rational, and detached, producing the rational white man in juxtaposition to an emotional Black one.[21]

Documentary as Training

There is a symbiosis between the form of the documentary and the governance of emotion through media culture about the history of U.S. chattel slavery. Derived from *documentum* (a lesson), the word *documentary* connotes an instructional form easily adaptable in the service of affective governance.[22] Documentaries are grounded in an assumption of truth, where images are considered evidentiary and provide supposedly unmediated access to reality. As such, documentary film gleans much of its discursive power from the presumption of direct access to the "real."[23] The conflation of documentary with unmediated truth is particularly acute in relation to television documentary, which derived authority during the 1960s in contrast to what Newton Minow famously called the "vast wasteland of television"; television documentary stood out as a voice of reason in the otherwise fictional televisual landscape.[24]

Almost exclusively addressed to a white, male, middle-class viewer—mirroring the racial and gender coding of the documentary form—the programs marginalized large segments of the audience and relied chiefly on white male experts.[25] For instance, although "The Heritage of Slavery" featured many interviews with both Black women and Black men, John McKnight, the Midwest director of the U.S. Civil Rights Commission, is brought in toward the end of the film as a (white) voice of reason to explain Black anger. The segments with McKnight, who became a Northwestern University professor in 1969, are a sharp contrast to earlier interviews with white southerners, who are featured as part of the southern landscape through footage of them on porches and in fields. McKnight, however, is interviewed in an office lined with books, which further adds to his authority. In 1965, A. William Bluem noted that by its fifth year, "*CBS Reports* had brought before the American public nearly 400 of the thinkers and doers of the world. Presidents, statesmen, scholars, and specialists from a dozen walks of life were sought out and recorded as they gave their opinions on matters relevant to the conduct and progress of our society."[26] Such "thinkers and doers of the world" were almost exclusively white men. Securing influence through the use of experts, documentary draws on a putatively neutral narrator to shore up claims to truth and objectivity through distance.

This claim to neutrality obfuscates what Gareth Palmer describes as documentary's role in providing "us ways of thinking"; I suggest that documentary similarly offers us ways of feeling.[27]

In other words, documentary is authoritative—especially so in this era—making it particularly suited to shaping and containing emotion in the service of shifting racial formations. Amid the upheaval of the 1960s, the documentaries attempted to restore order in part by working to reconstitute whiteness as antiracist. This reconstruction of whiteness is bound up with official antiracism, where national progress is yoked to the eradication of what was constituted by 1960's "Cast the First Stone," the first production of ABC's *Bell & Howell Close-Up!* series, as individual "prejudice" and "hate." In the documentary, discourses about modernity are articulated to whiteness and subjectivity, where being "enlightened" and modern means identifying and eliminating any discriminatory thoughts, feelings, or behaviors in order to be an ideal liberal citizen-subject. The connection to the state's official antiracism is made apparent in the January 20, 1961, Senate session, during which Senator William Proxmire (D-WI) asked that the entire transcript of "Cast the First Stone" be included in the congressional record. Using television's broad reach as justification, Proxmire underscored the medium's capacity as a tool of racial enlightenment: "Mr. President, television smashes into the public consciousness as no other media can. When it wishes to touch the public heart and mind by the millions, there is nothing, and has been nothing, like it. Television's capacity to heighten understanding of controversial social issues was strikingly illustrated recently by the ABC network program 'Cast the First Stone.' This program explored the subject of prejudice and discrimination in the Northern United States."[28]

For Proxmire, television is not a subtle or quiet way to influence, but rather it smashes into public consciousness and is singular in its ability to engender sympathy and effect understanding. Its scope is wide; as Proxmire notes, "Cast the First Stone" highlights "dislikes, hatreds, biases, and prejudices" across the nation.[29] Since its inception, television has been a technology of governance, one that drew together otherwise disparate sectors of the "governing classes" who were interested in the medium's possibilities as a tool for "inculcating the values of liberal capitalist democracy" to a mass audience.[30]

Simply put, television offered a platform from which to activate and engage citizens. The contested racial order of the 1960s meant that television documentary operated in the service of official antiracism, working to modify thoughts and behaviors in relation to race. A powerful cultural technology, the documentary provides a means to help resolve the so-called social issue of racism and white supremacy (understood by Proxmire and "Cast the First Stone" as discrimination and prejudice) by changing hearts and minds. This discourse of prejudice existing in the heart as well as the mind relies on affect as much as reason.

Prejudice, Shame, and Hatred

White shame about slavery and racism is not pathologized by "Cast the First Stone." Instead, white shame is considered the basis for self-examination to ensure that all remnants of "prejudice" have been eliminated so that national progress is not impeded by the "ugly face of prejudice in the north."[31] "Cast the First Stone" begins with an image of the white narrator, John Daly, obscured by darkness. As Daly speaks, he is literally enlightened from the shadows, and eventually his face is visible as he begins his narration:

> In darkness, prejudice is born. The father is ignorance. The mother, fear. The child, a life misshapen by hate. In our time, mankind condemns violence and hate, but there is in most of us a vestige of the savage past. And ironically, most of us hating have been hated in return. . . . The wonder of this nation is that its new freedoms, its ever new frontiers, and its bright confidence, have always in time raised these—the tired, the poor, the huddled masses—to dignity and a new estate.[32]

Theorizing racism as "prejudice" yields an individual and interpersonal framework and solution: instruction and knowledge must combat the flourishing of prejudice. Using racialized language, Daly describes the past as "savage" (and within the self), whereas the enlightened present is characterized by a disavowal of "violence and hate," an indication of tolerance that marks the subject as modern.[33] Downplaying the pervasiveness and gravity of white supremacy, "prejudice" reduces the scale and scope of the former, erasing the need for structural changes. Daly continues, narrating prejudice as collectively shameful:

> Our shame, and theirs, must be that they in turn have made those who have followed after the lowly, the despised, and the unwanted. For some, dignity, a new estate, and too often the illusion of superiority are won after bitter struggle in this never-ending conflict that through the years have marched the legions of every race, creed, and color. Chinese, Irish, Catholic, Jew, Italian, free-thinker, Pole, Latin American, and out of the bondage of slavery, the Negro.[34]

The shame here, our shame, is marked as both individual shame and the shame of the nation for continuing a cycle of conflict that purportedly implicates everyone. Rendering equivalent the experiences of various groups migrating to the United States, Daly also translates race into ethnicity and religion, expunging whiteness in order to describe those who struggled to assimilate into the nation at different historical moments.[35] This cannot be detached from the strengthening of the boundaries of whiteness, with those who were not considered white in earlier eras—"Finns, Hebrews, Slavs, and Greeks"—gradually assimilating into whiteness during the 1950s.[36] At the same time, the dichotomy between whiteness and Blackness was cemented to such an extent that the dominant understanding of race in the United States became further entrenched as "Black" and "white." The category "ethnicity" came to replace "race," resulting in an understanding of whiteness as innocent and detached from white supremacy; this maneuver worked as a "universalizing appeal to the underlying sameness of humanity and to the assimilative powers of American culture."[37] Most centrally, whiteness is defined in contrast to Blackness, where whiteness is solidified because it is not Black.

Daly briefly acknowledges slavery (and therefore the different histories of Irish Americans and African Americans) and implicitly connects Black struggle to this history:

> For the Negro, the struggle has been the hardest, the issue clearest drawn. The white south, the historic battleground for

the American Negro, has heard strident and accusing from
every other corner of the nation the cry "shame, shame." That
there is prejudice and discrimination in the south is beyond
question. But in full measure, north of the Mason-Dixon line,
its ugly shadow lies across city and countryside.[38]

Again, the word *shame* is used—for northern liberals, the south is a
blight on a modern nation intent on eradicating discrimination. Yet
as Daly continues, the north is where "subterfuge and expedience,
for instance, have built the new ghettos. The faces of prejudice are
many. Some are transparently ugly. Most piously benign. Its forms
are sometimes flagrant, most often subtle. Its sound is on some occa-
sions muted. On others, raucous."[39] With this, the documentary cuts
to footage of "American Nazi" George Rockwell yelling about the
demise of the United States and "the white race." Despite the immediate jump to an overt white supremacist, Daly's opening narration
implicitly critiques northern liberals—some "faces" of prejudice are
"piously benign"—and extends the quasi-religious undertone of the
program. In keeping with the discourse of prejudice as hidden, Daly
understands northern racism as shadowy and elusive, something that
must be illuminated; television is uniquely positioned as a tool of enlightenment that can help to ease the nation's shame. Although the
documentary problematizes white racial liberalism, this is softened
by the emphasis on shared complicity through the language of "discrimination," "prejudice," and "sin." In this way, everyone is incrimi-
nated, including the "victims" of prejudice themselves. By recasting
white supremacy, settler colonialism, and the afterlife of slavery as
solely issues of discrimination, prejudice, and hate, "Cast the First
Stone" offers liberal solutions and emphasizes hope and progress.

Such solutions involve training to eradicate prejudice, including
at universities "throughout the country" featuring classes in human
relations "to help in the fight against prejudice." Daly describes a
Jewett City, Connecticut, Baptist camp, where "a gathering of young
people . . . hear of how rumor breeds hate, from a guest, Rabbi Ar-
thur Gilbert." The camera cuts to Gilbert demonstrating the activity:
"This game is called rumor clinic. I will show you a picture and you
are to look at the picture." Over footage of young, white students,
Daly narrates, "The game: one person studies the picture, relates his

impression to the second and so on. Through subconscious distortions that razor is usually switched from the hand of the white man to that of the Negro."[40] Because prejudice is framed as subconscious, it requires special guidance in order to be revealed. Once it is exposed, the prejudiced white subject—not pathologized as sick with racism—must remain vigilant to recognize internalized stereotypes that could lead to discriminatory behavior.

During a particularly revealing moment, Daly explains that even the police are receiving training: "In police departments across the nation, officers are going back to school, learning that as guardians of the law, they must not be prejudicial nor discriminatory." The documentary shifts to footage of Detroit police academy instructor Roy Dickinson addressing a room of white police officers to explain the rationale for tackling racism, figured here as hatred and prejudice:

> The very security of the democratic way of life resides in effective safeguards against the loosening of racial, religious, and nationalistic hatreds. It follows then that you, police officers, must be ever alert against the irrational and emotional incitements of race baiters and religious bigots.[41]

Described as "irrational" and "emotional," race baiters are implicitly coded as Black, and the "democratic way of life"—white life—requires security and protection from Black anger and Black nationalism. Containing Black rage is presented as a requirement for the continuance of white life and its attendant racial formation. By instructing the police to be vigilant about "irrational and emotional incitements," Dickinson indicates that there is a proper way to deal with race—in this case, by separating whiteness from "racial hatred" and irrationality. White supremacy is left unaddressed, and, through thinly veiled language, Dickinson instructs the police to continuously surveil and monitor those "race baiters" who constitute a threat. By couching this order within the language of protecting democracy, Dickinson reproduces a progressive discourse present throughout the four documentaries: white liberal citizen-subjects must be aware, nonprejudiced, and versed in how to properly discuss race from a distanced, nonemotional position. "Cast the First Stone" thus makes visible the relationship between containment and production: Black rage must be quelled in order to produce white life and white rationality. Such emotional containment aligns with and supports official antiracism and its shifting racial order, which Daly underscores in his concluding narration: "In our Declaration of Independence with its emphasis on equality, the foundation of a way of life was laid. It is just as valid today as it was then. In a sense, even more so. The world today lives in the thunder of an insistent drumming demand for equality, sounded as never before." Seemingly in order to address glaring contradictions around inequality and race in the United States, Daly emphasizes that a "way of life"—that only some have been able to experience—has not been available to all. He continues, "There are practical arguments that should persuade us to honor our birthright: one, a presidential committee, for instance, estimates that discrimination costs $30 billion a year in wasted manpower, morale, and production. Two, on the world scene, it is clear that all hope for decency and the rights of man depend on the achievement of a firm enduring partnership between the free and the newly free nations of Africa and Asia." According to the documentary, there are material reasons to end discrimination, yet Daly argues that capital alone is not enough to persuade people to change, nor is an emphasis on the imperial aims of the United States with respect to Africa and Asia sufficiently persuasive. Rather, one must closely self-examine in order to end discrimination: "Yes, there are practical arguments against prejudice and discrimination. But its elimination is in the hearts and the minds of man. Let us then each, with the courage to be honest, look into our own hearts and minds. And only he that is without sin among you, let him cast the first stone."[42]

By rendering racism and white supremacy a matter of individual concern, the documentary urges viewers to search honestly their own "hearts and minds" for evidence of prejudice and discrimination, promulgating an individualized set of behaviors to address racism. The phrase "hearts and minds" also implies an emotional response; as Daly notes, rational facts—"practical arguments"—are insufficient to convince viewers to change, which contradicts documentary's overall impulse to effect social change through distanced commentary. Emphasizing the centrality of feeling to combating prejudice reveals the false dichotomy between reason and emotion on which the documentaries relied. As I demonstrate in the next chapter, *Roots* and its attendant curricula draw upon and bolster this discourse of an emotional answer to racism.

"Cast the First Stone" thus takes up the mantle of official antiracism by promoting a white racial formation that asks for minimal self-awareness to eradicate individual prejudice while preserving existing white life. This, in turn, is bound up with the nation and capital, as the progression of both requires a cursory examination of racism. For the good of the nation overall, prejudice and discrimination must be identified and eliminated using available tools; group training, the university, and television documentaries are presented as means for white people to enlighten themselves, abolish prejudice, and become modern. The construction of racism as an "increasingly illegible phenomenon in U.S. society, the unfortunate past that was gradually receding" goes hand in hand with the state's repurposing of minority difference "as an opportunity for power."[43] The preface to "The Heritage of Slavery," featuring Xerox president C. Peter McCullough, makes a similar argument: "This program will explore some of the things that white Americans and black Americans think about each other. How we think about each other is a matter of urgent concern because it affects how we act. To help blacks and whites achieve a better understanding, Xerox is sponsoring a series of seven programs, using the medium of television, to reach the widest possible audience."[44] The documentaries evince a presumed connection between "understanding"—enlightenment—and action, though it is action limited to certain realms and outlets, such as personal behavior. In lieu of systemic change, economic redistribution, and reparations, one must change one's heart and mind. Ideal liberal citizens, especially those in supposedly racism-free places (i.e., the north), must do the work of ridding themselves of prejudice in order to maintain a national harmony, one that ultimately perpetuates a slightly altered status quo, marked by racial politesse instead of street protest. In an interview, Wolff explains that he intended *Of Black America* "to change the language of the current racial dialogue by showing that racial trouble stems from historic attitudes—an inheritance of ignorance."[45] By making racism an issue of mind, the disease discourse functions as another mode of Black pathologization, claiming racism as in the head, not the culture at large.

Black Anger, White Fear

Constructing whiteness as rational and calm in contrast to an irrational and excessive Blackness was especially apparent in the ways that the television documentaries produced and augmented white fear of Black anger and violence. White fears about Black insurrection and uprising were rife on screen. The *Bell & Howell Close-Up!* episode "Walk in My Shoes" (1961) begins with a warning from the white narrator to white viewers that connects fears of communism to internal racial struggle: "This is no communist speaking. This is an angry Black man speaking. The twenty million black men of America are angry. America won't have to worry about communism. It'll have to worry about the restless black peril here in America."[46] The characterization of "twenty million black men" as a "peril" marks a space and population that is beyond recuperation and assistance; the restless Black peril is an endless, cyclical disease, a pathology for which white people have no responsibility. At stake for white viewers, then, is a continuous threat to white life if moderate concessions are not made and Black militancy is not quelled. In other words, the "*reason* white viewers should press for further civil rights reform is that without it, militant black movements will continue to grow."[47]

Such white anxiety about an intensifying Black militancy was augmented by the documentaries. In "Cast the First Stone," footage of Dick Gregory is followed by Daly's claims about Black humor, which he calls "wry": "[It is] born out of adversity but today it is apt to be edged with bitterness. There is an increasing ferment, a rising militancy among negroes not only in the south, where the recent sit-ins have had such a shattering impact, but in the north, where the negro is increasingly articulate about social and economic, as well as legal, equality." Through the use of language like "rising," "shattering," and "militancy," Daly paints a frightening picture for white viewers, which continues over a photo of Elijah Muhammad: "At one end of the spectrum is hate, born of hate. The black supremacy of Elijah Muhammad, a religious opportunist who has fired an estimated quarter of a million negroes with a hatred for the whites."[48] In one fell swoop, Daly reduces critiques of white supremacy to "hatred for the whites" wherein a Black demagogue, not the injustices of white supremacy, is the cause of hatred. The particular emphasis on figures like Muhammad and Stokely Carmichael rather than the larger movements of which they were a part occludes the fact that these movements were large, varied, and transnational.

The pathologization of Blackness thus extended to an affective domain, where anger, when racialized as Black, was cast as mental instability.[49] The inability to completely contain minoritized subjects' anger engendered new discourses to theorize and ultimately manage what Amber Jamilla Musser calls "unruly subjects, who disrupt the passive suffering that sympathy and empathy require." Anger, by contrast, does not elicit guilt, and angry subjects are threatening.[50] Differing from the "damage imagery" used with the intention to "dismantle the racial system," Black rage imagery was an attempt by liberal intellectuals to "convey to whites that blacks were no longer willing to accept the status quo."[51] In the late 1960s, Black psychiatrists William H. Grier and Price M. Cobbs published *Black Rage,* offered as a liberal interpretation of the uprisings of the era.[52] According to Daryl Michael Scott, the book "represented the attempt of two integrationists to counter the nationalist trend in the black movement and the white backlash" by highlighting how Black anger "is frightening to white America."[53] Black nationalism, in particular, was considered a psychosis and could therefore be discredited through its depiction as an "outgrowth of personality problems"—a follower of Muhammad, for instance, "was an irrational type who knew the truth 'with his heart rather than his mind.'"[54] Simultaneously, schizophrenia was recodified as a "Black disease," one characterized by anger, hostility, and violence.

Jonathan Metzl has extensively detailed how schizophrenia, once considered a disease affecting (unthreatening) white, middle-class women, became connected to Black masculinity during the 1960s. Metzl points to a 1968 article by psychiatrists Walter Bromberg and Franck Simon that "described schizophrenia as a 'protest psychosis' whereby black men developed 'hostile and aggressive feelings' and 'delusional anti-whiteness' after listening to the words of Malcolm X, joining the Black Muslims, or aligning with groups that preached militant resistance to white society." Bromberg and Simon argued that these men required psychiatric treatment because of the threat they posed not just to themselves but also to the "social order of white America."[55] According to Bromberg and Simon, protesting made Black men crazy, and they were also crazy for protesting. In this way, Blackness and protesting against racism were co-constructed as features of insanity.[56]

The very title of 1963's *CBS Reports* episode "The Harlem Temper" underscores white anxieties about Black mood, characterized as a "temper" that might be lost. Featuring Black activists with a range of politics—from the Congress of Racial Equality (CORE) and the NAACP to Elijah Muhammad and Malcolm X—the program operates as a warning to white viewers about what will happen if moderate measures are not taken. Despite a stated emphasis on encouraging understanding as a means toward equality, the documentaries focused little on promoting understanding about Black life and instead produced white fears about perceived threats to white life and white space. In effect, the documentaries had a contradictory function of both creating white fear while also reassuring white viewers of the existence of moderate Black activism geared toward more reformist goals. "The Harlem Temper," in particular, used the work of organizations like CORE and the NAACP as foils for more threatening activism. After featuring civil rights groups working to effect change through legal channels and education (rather than a cultural transformation), narrator Harry Reasoner emphasizes the ever-present threat of militancy, implying that Black communities are open to capture by radical groups: "Most negroes in Harlem have not yet been brought into the civil rights fight. Black Muslims are filling the vacuum by moving among those negroes at the bottom of the social and economic ladder with phenomenal success. Through a kind of racism in reverse, they hold their followers by giving them a sense of dignity in being black." Reasoner goes on to claim Harlem as the "mecca" for Black Muslims and emphasizes that although their membership is "secret . . . it is estimated to be higher than 100,000 nationally." Reasoner treats Black nationalism similarly, noting that it also "fills the void in Harlem."[57] The speeches of Lewis Michaux and Elijah Muhammad are featured as worthy or important not because of their content but rather because of the threats to white life contained within them—in other words, as

pieces of inflammatory rhetoric. Nationalism and pride are demon-
ized and threatening when racialized as Black.

Black Insurrection and White Anxiety

The history of U.S. chattel slavery alternately haunts the documentaries and at times is made explicit by them as the root cause of
Black anger in the 1960s. There is thus a contradiction between a
progress narrative that understands slavery as located elsewhere—
the past—and slavery's haunting of the present as an explanation of
Black rage.[58] Slavery is suggested as providing the blueprint for Black
resistance, while simultaneously, the afterlife of slavery—slavery's
continuing effects on contemporary everyday life—is also provided
as the reason for present-day struggle.[59] This is particularly visible in
"The Harlem Temper" when Reasoner explains that Black separat-
ism and nationalism originated under slavery:

> The lure of Africa is not a new thing for the American Negro.
> It goes back to the early slave revolts against the slave system
> of the old south. Before the Civil War, in the 1850s, the first
> forms of Negro nationalism developed out of the social
> unrest among the free slaves in the north, calling for Afro-
> Americans to leave this country.[60]

Historicizing Black nationalism, Reasoner underscores the fact that
northern freedom is not sufficient. At the same time, Reasoner modifies "the south" with the adjective "old," using a temporal marker to
locate slavery in the past. He continues, explaining a "second burst"
in the 1920s, when Marcus Garvey "galvanized Negro discontent in
a Back-to-Africa campaign that enveloped tens of thousands of Negroes before the movement collapsed." Using words like "lure" and
"enveloped," Black nationalists and separatists are rendered suscep-
tible dupes, easily attracted to movements constructed by the documentary as irrational and ineffective, yet that somehow still persist.[61]
Within the hegemonic discourse of Black rage, such so-called irrational desires are the outgrowth of a diseased psyche filled with hate
and anger, which leads to emotional and excessive behavior. In 1969,
the historian Allen Matusow portrayed Black Power ideology as aris-

ing "not from the pursuit of freedom but from the avoidance of pain. There were no noble principles motivating black activists." According to the era's mainstream social science, Black radicals were "merely feeling organisms, emotional beings bereft of rational motives, who recoiled in pain and groped for therapy."[62] Without "rational motives" in a racialized social order privileging "rationality" (and constructing the category as completely and necessarily separate from emotion), Black activists could be easily dismissed as ill and damaged.

Yet despite this dismissal, Black anger was still constructed as a very real threat, one that "The Heritage of Slavery" allegorically connected to the history of slavery as the source of contemporary radical and revolutionary resistance. States narrator George Foster, "Today, all over America, there are still echoes of the noises made when one race tries to subjugate another. On this broadcast, we will explore the heritage of slavery and the roots of Black rebellion."[63] By emphasizing enslaved resistance, "The Heritage of Slavery" responds to apologists for slavery who declare that enslaved people were content and compliant; at the same time, the documentary taps into white fears of Black insurrection and revolution by claiming the heritage of slavery as Black rebellion rather than ongoing white supremacist modes of thought and resource distribution. Here the documentary makes visible long-standing white anxiety about repercussions for slavery.[64] Over a shot of fences in Charleston, Foster narrates:

> Like other immigrants to America, the slaves were huddled masses. But unlike the others, what Blacks were huddled against was America itself. Often, they rebelled. Quite often. Partly in order to deal with inside agitators, Charleston put walls and fences all over the place. Turns out, if you bought a slave, you may have bought yourself an insurrectionist.[65]

Foster draws on an emerging narrative about the United States as a nation of immigrants to distinguish enslaved Africans from immigrants, connecting enslaved resistance to revolt against the nation itself.[66] Yet Foster does not explicitly mark the difference as sourced in captivity for Africans; rather, he draws the distinction by constituting enslaved Africans as rebellious and against the United States, whereas "other immigrants" were simply huddled masses with no propensity for turning against the nation. Without explanation—there is no mention of white culpability for slavery or the fact that white people were the instigators and profiteers—Blackness is thus framed as revolutionary and against the state from the outset because of an unnamed state of captivity. By constituting enslaved people as "immigrants" and juxtaposing them with noninsurrectionist huddled masses, the presumption is that the anti-American "inside agitators" were incapable of acclimating to the United States. By contrast, the relationship between whiteness and rationality is presumed, where rational, detached white (male) citizens are not antagonistic to the state and are always fit for citizenship and belonging.

By producing and perpetuating white fear of Black violence, the documentaries educate white viewers about what is at stake—namely, white life. At the same time, Black violence is connected to slavery in both explicit and implicit ways. Teaching white viewers about slavery, then, has a contradictory function: the present is explained through discursive emphasis on the past, thereby attempting to locate slavery there, yet slavery clearly also possesses the present, visible in the living throwbacks threatening the modern United States.[67] The progress narrative attempted by the documentaries is interrupted by slavery's afterlife, made evident through the documentaries themselves. Despite white attempts to manage, direct, and edit Black voices and experiences as mediated by the documentaries, the afterlife of slavery is still a visible rupture.

A "Season of Revelation" for Whiteness

White fears about Black activism and resistance quickly morphed into resentment, perhaps never absent. Where "Cast the First Stone" asked white viewers to root out their prejudice, by the mid-1960s, "Black Power, White Backlash" suggested that white Americans were fed up. The success of the civil rights movement in using visual mediums to publicize white racial terror was temporary, with the 1960s marking the emergence of a growing backlash against representing Black victimhood. In its stead, a national discourse about a "crime problem" took hold, constructing "African Americans as threats to an American way of life that was implicitly understood to be white."[68]

The waning of white liberal support for the civil rights movement(s) is made a focal point of "Black Power, White Backlash." Beginning with footage of twenty-five-year-old Stokely Carmichael at a rally chanting, "We want Black Power!" the documentary turns to Wallace, who claims that the summer of 1966 "was a season of revelation for the white man in the north":

> For the first time, he began fully to comprehend the intensity of his feelings and his fears about the Black man. For years, he had watched, smug and fascinated, as the southern Black and white were played out for him like some morality play on his television screen. But he remained a spectator, only half involved. Then came summer 1966, and as riots crackled through his cities, the northern white man came to realize the depth of his confusion, his animosity, and fear. Black Power was the catalyst, a phrase shouted by a 25-year-old revolutionary on a Mississippi highway. It was a rallying cry to northern Blacks mired in frustration and bitterness. A cry that sounded like a threat of violence, of vengeance, to a white man fed up with racial turmoil.[69]

Here, Wallace points to the affective dimensions of white supremacy by noting that only now, when threatened by Black power, is the northern white man implicated in the racial drama supposedly limited to the southern United States. He is forced to reckon with his feelings (namely, fear), no longer able to view white racial terror as merely compelling theater. Wallace constructs this imagined northern white man (women are erased entirely) as exasperated and reasonable for being so, since now Black activism was reaching his own city. After detailing the aftermath of urban uprisings, Wallace concludes, "The most serious casualty of all was the relationship between the Black man and the white man. By summer's end, the northern white was counter-marching, counter-demonstrating." As with "The Heritage of Slavery," Wallace and "Black Power, White Backlash" reproduce long-standing white fears of Black revolution, embodied in "Black Power, White Backlash" by Carmichael.

Despite Carmichael's efforts to explain white supremacy and white terrorism against people of color, Wallace and the documentary continually produce Carmichael and Black power as irrational, violent threats to white life. Turning to Carmichael, Wallace states:

> When you talk of Black Power, building a movement that will smash everything that Western civilization has created, when you say that Black Power should bring the country to its knees anytime it messes with the Black man—and these are quotes from Stokely Carmichael—the picture has got to be, in the mind of white man and Black man, one of a man who threatens violence.[70]

Carmichael replies that Black men are in dire need of protection because they are not afforded it as citizens and so must form a collective movement. Carmichael goes on to detail incidents of white violence against Black men, which Wallace dismisses as exceptional and returns again to the question of violence as a tactic. Throughout, Wallace alternately condescends, argues with, and ignores Carmichael's points about power and the ongoing legacy of slavery. Carmichael notes, "I think that this country is run by property ownership and that black people are not only propertyless, they are viewed as property. We have to move to a position of property ownership in this country so that we can bargain from a position of strength with racists rather than a position of weakness." Wallace replies by pointing out that Carmichael went from a New York City ghetto to getting a good education. We can understand Carmichael as expressing what Stephen Best and Saidiya Hartman term "black noise," which refers to "the kinds of political aspirations that are inaudible and illegible because they are so wildly utopian and derelict to capitalism."[71] At the same time, the camerawork contributes to the framing of Carmichael as irrational. The documentary begins with close-ups of Carmichael, shot from below, at a protest. The effect is of a singular, angry man who looms over others, threatening in both his speech and presence. During his interview with Wallace, Carmichael is in his office, but his books are excluded from the frame. When we see him and Wallace together, Wallace is in the far left of the frame, with Carmichael in the bottom right, shot from behind. We do not see

Carmichael's face, and the effect is of a calm teacher (Wallace) lecturing a petulant student (Carmichael).

Throughout the documentary, the continued emphasis on violence works to detract from the very reasons violence might be used as a tactic. Wallace interviews leaders from various ends of the political spectrum, from Martin Luther King Jr. to more radical activists like Carmichael and Dan Watts, asking each about violent struggle. The narrative fixation on violence underscores white fears while also contributing to them, yet simultaneously, Daniel Patrick Moynihan is featured as a rational counterpoint to the anger of Carmichael and Watts. Filmed in his office, Moynihan is shot in such a way that his books are visible in the frame, lending him an air of authority. Furthermore, he is interviewed halfway through the documentary and set up as the calm interlocutor who can explain Carmichael, Watts, and Martin Luther King Jr. to an audience in need of Moynihan's translation and his ability to "assess Negro leaders and Negro attitudes."[72] Watts, Carmichael, and King cannot speak for themselves but rather need a rational white man to interpret their beliefs and to help white viewers understand. Asked about their impact, Moynihan replies:

> Well, I would hope that we would think there's something to hope for from a Stokely Carmichael and a Dan Watts. Now, they use a vocabulary that's pretty discouraging, pretty disrupting. People get excited, whites get upset. Well, they want you to get upset! [Chuckles.] Whoever met a 26-year-old social reformer who didn't want you to get upset about what he had to say to you. But the things that Dan Watts asks for are not things that a person shouldn't be asking for. They aren't things he isn't entitled to. A man like Dan Watts is a skilled, trained architect, a university man, an American citizen. All he's saying is give me and give us what is by rights the situation of any American. Or if you don't, you're going to have trouble. But we don't need the trouble, we can give him what he's asking for.

Wallace responds by bringing the conversation back to violence: "[Watts] says that he will disrupt American society if it means blowing manhole covers or possibly derailing trains or sniping or whatever until the white man comes to the bargaining table and negotiates—buys peace from the Black man." Blackness is reproduced as threatening and violent while "Black Power, White Backlash" simultaneously seeks to contain the threat by dismissing the power of Black nationalism. Indeed, Moynihan reassures viewers that Martin Luther King Jr. is "much more in keeping with the political and moral traditions of the negro American" than Carmichael or Watts.[73]

Quantifying Feelings

Documentary's privileging of rationality over emotion is especially evident at the end of "Black Power, White Backlash," which turns toward the positivism of statistics and data as the true measure of what is happening in the United States. The documentary concludes with Wallace interviewing Louis Harris, a white man and "one of this nation's foremost public opinion analysts," about the changes in the "northern white man's attitudes toward the Black man" after the summer of 1966. Over a visual of poll numbers, Harris explains that more whites now consider the pace of the civil rights movement too fast. In the pared-down space of the studio, Harris is produced as the voice of rationality with recourse to fact, evidenced in statistical data, but critically, the evidence is white people's feelings. Such supposed proof via the logic of the polls positions Harris as the ultimate authority, bolstered by him having the last say to end the documentary. When asked about violence, Harris notes, "Well the demonstrations I think would not have had this impact if it hadn't been for the fear that whites have over the violence of riots that have taken place in negro ghettos in the northern cities and in fact in Atlanta and some southern cities."[74]

After showing a slide, he explains that when broken down by income, "You find that hardly more than a third of the low-income white people in this country are convinced the negroes are not violent." Wallace follows up by asking, "Which negro demands breed the most hostility?" Harris responds by listing integrated neighborhoods and housing as the "deepest fear that bounds in white society today." No longer considered worthy of sympathy, Black subjects are constructed as having lost white goodwill due to irrational and excessive rage. Along these lines, to answer Wallace's question about where the "so-called white liberal" stands at the end of the summer, Harris notes a dramatic shift: "Back in 1963, two out of every three white, college-educated liberal people, mainly in the north, were in sympathy to the Civil Rights Movement. On the eve of this summer . . . you found just about 50 percent of these white liberals who were sympathetic, a slippage, but at the end of this summer, it's scarcely more than one in four who feel sympathetic any longer. There's been a disenchantment among your white liberals with the Civil Rights Movement."[75]

"Black Power, White Backlash" uses the loss of white liberal support as one of the stakes of violence, with former supporters flocking to and shoring up whiteness in the face of profound threats to white life. The emphasis on northern white liberals in "Black Power, White Backlash," "The Harlem Temper," and other TV documentaries of the era aligns with Aniko Bodroghkozy's characterization of 1960s news and entertainment programming on race, which "encouraged audiences to engage self-reflexively with 'Northern' and 'Southern' categories of regional identity, as well as categories of 'blackness' and 'whiteness.'"[76] White viewers—even northern liberal ones—are hailed by "Black Power, White Backlash" to identify with the critique of Black militancy. During his concluding narration, Wallace calls for moderation: "Edmund Burke has said the only thing necessary for the triumph of evil is for good men to do nothing. If the methods of the extremists, Black and white, are not eventually to prevail, then the rest of the community, Black and white, the *vast* majority, must come together now to solve this American dilemma."[77]

Solving the "Problem" of Race

Although television documentaries devoted to race and civil rights issues waned during the mid-1960s, the Kerner Commission Report was central in the surge of documentary programs on "issues" in 1968.[78] President Johnson's response to the civil unrest of 1967, the Kerner Report connected Black disenfranchisement and urban degradation to white racism and white life. Television documentary once again took up the questions of race, emotion, and national belonging after being urged to do so. Network executives met with government officials who advocated for the networks "to devote more coverage to black problems," which were constituted as particularly salient after the assassination of Martin Luther King Jr. and "the national wave of racial violence it precipitated."[79] The construction of Blackness as irrational, angry, and violent provided a blueprint for idealized whiteness as calm, rational, and reasonable by contrast; the documentaries played a key role in this formation.[80]

CBS's documentary *Of Black America* can be situated as part of this renewed push for programming concerning race and a putative emphasis on Black life. At the same time, this series aligns with official antiracism and capitalism's uptake of minority difference in the service of profit. Airing in 1968, *Of Black America* was sponsored by the Xerox Corporation, which spent $1 million to air the series without commercial interruption.[81] Responding to questions about the effectiveness of the investment (and how one might measure the response), vice president of corporate communications David Curtin pointed to mail as the only yardstick: "To date, Xerox has received 1,697 letters, of which it finds 1,468 favorable and 229 unfavorable, a ratio of about 7.5 to 1 supporting the project." One viewer in particular, a "New York stockholder," wrote that the sponsorship was "'not only good business but good politics in the best sense.'" The network estimated that twenty-two million viewers had "seen all or part of the documentary."[82] According to a 1968 *New Republic* article, *Of Black America* constituted the only "serious" response to the Kerner Report: "Richard Salant, president of CBS News, told me that the network decided to do something after a talk with the Kerner Commission in Poughkeepsie last November. 'The most manageable thing,' Salant said, 'was to do a series on the black heritage.' When I asked why CBS wasn't doing anything to restore dialogue between the races, Salant said dialogue 'would harden positions [already taken], and be repetitious.' 'We want to get the unchurched,' he added."[83] After two of the seven documentaries aired, Doris Innis (identified in the article as wife of CORE director Roy Innis) wrote a review of the series for *Life*, calling it a "flawed breakthrough on blackness." She noted her impulse to "praise CBS to the skies for a major breakthrough. . . . God knows it is far above the usual TV fare." But she also critiqued the series, "the first two programs, at least," for either "[avoiding] dangerous ground or [making] only delicate tracks across it."[84] The state and capital invested in making the documentaries as a response to racialized civil unrest.

Ultimately, the documentaries positioned themselves as "solutions" to what were constituted as the dual crises of threats to white life and escalating Black insurrection during the era. By connecting Black anger to slavery, the documentaries produced distance between the antebellum era and the current moment and located slavery in the past while simultaneously highlighting its ongoing effects—namely, the threat of Black rage. As George Foster noted in his concluding narration to "The Heritage of Slavery":

> It's a long way and a lot of years from the slave market in Charleston to the Wall of Respect in Chicago, but neither distance nor time has yet entirely separated the Black man from bondage. No one needs to inflame the Black race against these realities. The fire of rebellion started burning a long time ago. What these travails in Black America have shown is that white racism created the need for Black Power, just as slavery bred insurrection.[85]

Here, modern-day "white racism" is severed from "slavery." These concessions work to establish distance from the overt racism now considered passé while also constraining more radical possibilities.

At the same time, the television documentaries relied on the seriousness of the genre to further bolster their claims to truth and rationality in the face of racialized chaos and emotion. In so doing, they offered a template for white subjects to address "discrimination" in calm and rational ways, and sometimes through affective responses carefully managed within the frame of expertise. Whiteness was thus shored up as rational and innocent; Blackness, in turn, was constituted as irrational, excessive, and threatening, in the documentaries themselves as well as within the broader discourse of pathologized Black anger to which the documentaries contributed. Describing white support for the 1964 Civil Rights Act, Amber Jamilla Musser argues that through the production of distance from Black suffering, white Americans "could objectify and separate blackness and simultaneously produce themselves as virtuous subjects."[86] For white viewers, eradicating prejudice was suggested as a way to contain such threats to whiteness. The rational and authoritative medium provided white audiences a way to deal with the shame of slavery by locating slavery in the past and separating it from whiteness. In essence, this temporal move to address shame engaged with slavery as lessons, fact, and pedagogy through the documentary form. Documentary provided an authoritative and supposedly unbiased distance in dealing with the history of slavery logically rather than through emotion—Black anger, in particular, was a threat the documentaries worked to contain. In the next chapter, I turn to the absorbing melodramatic form and the question of Black shame.

CHAPTER 2

Feeling Slavery: *Roots* and
Pedagogies of Emotion

Discussion continues over the relative impacts of the
television series, the Alex Haley novel, and the timing of their
release. One point is undeniably clear: "Roots" has touched
more Americans than any previous social or educational
phenomenon.

Educators have found "Roots" to be a rarity. As a
cognitive learning experience, "Roots" represents a major
contribution to black American history. As an affective
learning experience, the story of the Haley family strikes
an emotional chord appreciable by all students.

—Miami-Dade Community College promotional brochure

The ruptures around race, violence, and white supremacy during the 1960s made it difficult—though not impossible—for white Americans to ignore the profound social and political transformations taking place on a global scale. As demonstrated in the previous chapter, television documentaries on race, slavery, and civil rights struggles both produced white fears of racial upheaval and assuaged them by working to reassure white viewers that white life could be protected through slight concessions to activist demands. Within the periodization of post–civil rights, it is necessary to attend to how racial formations similarly underwent significant shifts—whiteness, in particular, was tenacious and adaptive even in the face of sustained activism and trenchant critique. In this chapter, I suggest that it became important to *feel* in ways that aligned with broader changes taking place in terms of the state's shift to official antiracism and the attendant fluctuations in the production of whiteness and Blackness.

By the 1970s, the tension between a statistical and detached approach to racism and an emotional one attentive to changing one's feelings tilted toward the latter. The enthusiasm for an emotional response to racism and the history of U.S. chattel slavery is made especially plain in the discourse surrounding the 1977 television miniseries *Roots,* which told the story of a family enduring slavery over the span of two hundred years. At the time of its airing, *Roots* was deemed capable of providing healing for a nation constructed as in need of catharsis in the wake of the 1960s. In 1977, Vernon Jordan, executive director of the National Urban League, referred to *Roots* as "the single most spectacular educational experience in race relations in America."[1]

The historical context of the 1970s and the shift from the radical ethos of the 1960s is significant here: The U.S. Bicentennial, an interest in genealogy (supported by the state via the Ethnic Heritage Studies Act of 1974), and an emphasis on lifestyle and identity combined to produce a *Roots* curriculum around slavery that pulled from the melodramatic form to underscore progress, inclusion, identity, and the liberal multicultural individual, even as the Bicentennial was haunted by slavery. Moreover, the rise of multiculturalism offered a means to quell dissent by promoting understanding, admiration, and appreciation. Racial harmony, in other words, could be achieved through ethnic pride, one that appropriated the rhetoric of Black pride espoused by the Black Power movements of the era. I argue that the series and its broader cultural uptake attempted to incorporate African Americans as part of the nation and to teach the proper feelings with respect to slavery and race for a new era and racial order: whereas the television documentaries sought to manage escalating Black insurrection through objectivity and distance, in this instance, television teaches viewers how to feel about U.S. chattel slavery and its ongoing legacies.

Documentary offered an authoritative and putatively unbiased way to deal with the history of slavery logically rather than through emotion—Black anger, in particular, was a threat the documentaries sought to contain. By contrast, in this chapter I show how educational curricula based on *Roots* emphasized rather than downplayed emotion. Through a focus on emotion, *Roots* and the curricula work as a form of sentimental education, where one learns the "range of appropriate social expressions of feeling."[2] I contend that this emotional management is part of an ongoing shift to official antiracism throughout the 1970s, during which the academy, state, and capital drew on minority difference for particular aims: rather than focusing primarily on repression, these institutions began viewing minority difference as productive for power.[3] I suggest that sentimental education constitutes one way that minoritized subjects were both incorporated and disciplined. At the same time, sentimental education contributed to the reshaping of whiteness in the 1970s, as seen in the push to learn and adopt particular feelings and emotional states with respect to issues of slavery, race, and racism. In what follows, I underscore the centrality of emotion to racial formation and the production of racialized subjectivity. Whereas 1960s documentaries emphasized thinking and behaving differently to uproot prejudice, the *Roots* curricula emphasizes feeling differently. Such instruction in feeling is visible not only in the text of *Roots* itself but also in the pedagogy developed to ensure that viewers internalized particular lessons. Black viewers are encouraged to feel pride as a way to overcome shame, while white viewers are taught admiration for Black struggle and sympathy for African Americans. Instilling these proper emotions becomes a key part of constituting post–civil rights subjects whose antiracism aligns with and bolsters that espoused by the academy, state, and capital.

As noted in a Miami-Dade Community College packet to teachers about the college-level course, "'Roots' opened minds and doors to many avenues of learning. It reflected feelings bottled up for several centuries."[4] These feelings, revealed through the experience of the miniseries, are constituted by the curricula as prejudice requiring a change of heart. Although this framing shares similarities with the rhetoric of eradicating prejudice discussed in chapter 1, the melodramatic form of *Roots* emphasizes the act of feeling as a means to catharsis and closure. This affective focus on prejudice in turn occludes from view structural racism and the racialized flow of wealth in the United States, especially pertinent during the 1970s as neoliberal restructuring via deindustrialization left cities and communities in ruin. To manage feelings brought up by the miniseries, the curricula and larger discourse around *Roots* center pride and admiration rather than rage and shame as the acceptable emotions for a decade steeped in a changing notion of pride. Despite Miami-Dade

Community College's euphemistic appeal in a promotional brochure that "unlike some of the Black history curricula that have ex-
isted, 'Roots' popularity is strong throughout the broad spectrum of
the student body," it is important to note that some of the teachings
were divided along a Black/white color line, with an emphasis on
pride and shame for Black viewers.[5] For white viewers, the pedagogical focus was on cultivating sympathy and admiration for African
Americans.

Critically, the state participated in this project of inculcating ethnic pride, with the Bicentennial celebrations of 1976 promoting state-
sponsored heritage via "massive events that were funded and staged
by the state."[6] Events like the Festival of American Folklife emphasized ethnic diversity and connected that to American exceptional-
ism, claiming the United States as unique in its pluralistic society.[7]
Such celebrations, Glenda Carpio notes, combined with the "highly
publicized racial struggles" of the 1960s to provoke "a great deal of
reflection regarding the nation's history"; at the same time, the contradiction between a discourse of freedom and democracy and the
history of U.S. chattel slavery was made plain. As a result, during
this moment, slavery "assumed a central role in public discourses in
America."[8] Through *Roots*, the state and commercial television produced a literacy around slavery that attempted to incorporate African Americans into the nation.

Much of this work, I suggest, occurred through the deployment
and disciplining of feeling: namely, the management of Black rage
and white anxiety. By transferring the shame about slavery from its
ostensible location as the purview of white Americans and locating it
with Black Americans, the *Roots* curricula promotes a specific form
of Black pride based on genealogy and survivorship—a pride less
threatening to white supremacy than the politicized pride and anger
of the 1960s. Through *Roots* and its hero Kunta Kinte, the curricula argued, Black Americans should now feel pride in having survived slavery, where once they supposedly experienced only shame. Shame, in
this conception, holds Black Americans back from self-actualization
and full citizenship; as such, overcoming shame becomes a requisite for incorporation into both the nation and U.S. history. At the
same time, the Films Incorporated curricula's discussion of slavery
works to point out how far the United States has progressed since

the antebellum era, framing this distance specifically in terms of the "healing" that *Roots* is understood to facilitate. By writing a progress narrative featuring a heroic male ancestor, Alex Haley liberalizes the era's radical movements. He deploys a particular version of history as a means toward pride, one that erases the centrality of women as well as the pervasiveness of collective resistance to slavery. This progress narrative, present in much of the popular discourse as well, works at an affective level by managing Black anger and assuaging white guilt as a means toward "new racial understanding."[9] In this instance, the focus on managing emotion erases the material realities of white supremacy and obscures the possibility of rebellion.

The Educational Import of *Roots*

Based on Alex Haley's book and produced by David L. Wolper, *Roots* was both a television event and a cultural phenomenon, garnering more than 130 million viewers over its eight-night run. In addition to its record-breaking viewership, heretofore only outdone by the 1976 airing of David Selznick's film version of *Gone with the Wind,* the televised *Roots* conferred moral seriousness onto television and changed the medium itself through the miniseries format, which altered television's typical flow and aligned well with the sentimentality of the miniseries.[10] Cities across the country, from New York and Los Angeles to Gary, Indiana, and Davenport, Iowa, declared the week of January 23, 1977, to be "Roots Week."[11]

During its eight-night consecutive run, *Roots* introduced audiences to the hero Kunta Kinte, who was captured in Gambia as a teenager and sold to a slave trader. Although the series begins with somewhat lighthearted scenes of Kinte growing up (and includes an infamous scene featuring a cameo by O.J. Simpson, whose character runs after Kinte), the tone quickly shifts. Viewers watched as Kinte endures the harrowing and horrific trip across the Middle Passage, after which he is sold to enslaver Reynolds, who forces Kinte to take the name Toby. Kinte's insistence on keeping his own name and his desire for freedom forms the backbone of the narrative. Indeed, much of the series' affective and melodramatic pull comes from Kinte's attempts to resist and escape, and his never-ending dream of freedom, a dream that he transmits to his daughter, Kizzy. One of the most heartbreaking scenes occurs when Kizzy is sold away from Kinte and his wife, Bell. Like Kinte, Kizzy retains hope for freedom, and the remainder of the series tells the story of the generations between Kizzy and Alex Haley, emphasizing the continuous and generational longing for freedom. This desire is highlighted in the supplemental educational material, along with issues of loss and suffering framed through contemporary struggles for justice.

Although simply watching *Roots* was considered to be a first-rate educational experience, curricula based on the series were quickly developed to coincide with the airing of the miniseries. In conjunction with Alex Haley, Miami-Dade Community College drew on academics and other experts to produce a college-level curriculum, and Films Incorporated created elementary- and junior-high-level curricula. Founded in 1928 as one of the earliest distributors of 16mm films to the home market, Films Incorporated was sold in 1951 to Encyclopaedia Britannica Films and in 1968, under the leadership of Charles Benton, began acquiring television contracts. During the early 1970s, Benton and Gale Livengood, a former schoolteacher and principal who worked for Encyclopaedia Britannica Films during the 1950s, met with Wolper and his lawyer Erwin Russell "to renew Films Inc.'s non-theatrical distribution agreement." During this meeting, "Wolper . . . mentioned that he was in the process of creating a new series on black history that might also be of interest, comprising thirteen hours of material based on a historical book by a man named Alex Haley. When *Roots* finally aired . . . Films Inc. sold over a million dollars worth of 16mm prints from leads acquired from its television showing."[12]

Wolper was explicit about his pedagogical aims, claiming *Roots* as an "exciting educational experience told in a dramatic and educational form." In response to critics who charged *Roots* with being middlebrow pablum at best, Wolper stated that he intended to educate a mass audience through television, which "should be used as a mass cultural medium, not just to educate a chosen few—and the gigantic audience out there wants to be educated, but they want it their way. If they want to be educated in a 'Middle Brow' way by being entertained at the same time—so what!"[13] Wolper thus championed an "edutainment" approach, arguing that a mass audience wanted to be entertained as well as educated.[14] Using a man in a hard hat as an example of a typical unreachable pupil, Wolper noted in an interview with Robert Sklar:

> I say that hard hat wants to be informed; you've got to find out how to inform him; I'm telling you how to inform that man; that man learned more about slavery in 6 hours in TV than in 6000 books; you can teach anything on TV—you just have to make it entertaining.[15]

Wolper's remarks invoke what Julie Passanante Elman identifies as broader interest in edutainment during the 1970s, with "new pedagogical modes of storytelling" reshaping the landscape of popular culture with "realistic, socially relevant, and entertaining" fare.[16] Instead of a dry, detached, or somber approach, edutainment sought to captivate an audience through pleasure, drama, and sometimes even fun.

The widespread enthusiasm for *Roots* and its imagined possibilities was bolstered by the National Education Association (NEA), which heartily endorsed the series and worked with ABC to promote and distribute *Roots* across educational levels. Providing more than 500,000 high schools with "supplementary materials on the series," the NEA notified Wolper during April 1977 that "over 500,000 secondary (junior high school and high school) teachers made ROOTS a classroom assignment. This is in addition to the over 200 colleges that actually gave credit for the watching of ROOTS and the reading of the book—an official college program."[17] In a letter to Wolper during early production, Linley Stafford, manager of the NEA's Editorial Information Center, reported that he had met Dick Connolly, head of ABC's press operations, to discuss the NEA's involvement with *Roots*: "I plan a major campaign within the education community. Every one of our 1.8 million members will be aware of the broadcasts in time to plan in-class use of the programs. Since this is a series of broadcasts, I think we should change the recommendation which appears at the end of the broadcasts to something like: 'Roots' has been recommended by The National Education Association."[18] The NEA's support validated and endowed *Roots* and its curricula with educational authority.

Reshaping Black Pride

Shaping and managing emotion was central to the reformulation of race and racial formation in the wake of the 1960s, especially given the efforts by the state, capital, and the U.S. academy to incorporate minority difference during this era. Such maneuvers likewise cannot be separated from the broader shift to neoliberal governance during the 1970s. By disciplining and governing emotion alongside what Patricia Clough refers to as "affective or life capacities," difference could be productive for capital rather than disruptive of it.[19] In this way, fostering particular emotions and feelings was a means to render minority difference unthreatening.

The entanglement of affective governance, racial formation, and capital is present in the *Roots* curricula and its broader uptake, particularly with respect to pride and shame. In the 1978 Films Incorporated Teacher's Guide (for grade seven through college), the bullet-pointed rationales for why students should study *Roots* center on racialized uplift and dignity:

- It gives students the incentive to explore their own family histories and helps them to discover, in Alex Haley's words, "a sense of self, a sense of dignity, a sense of worth, and a sense of being part of."
- It has changed the image of the black past from something black Americans were ashamed of to something heroic which they can regard with pride.
- It has pointed out the sense of rootlessness felt by Americans of other ethnic backgrounds.[20]

Drawing a connection between an individual sense of self and being a part of a collective (the nation), the guide suggests that studying family history offers this belonging and, further, assumes an a priori desire for belonging. The presumption of Black shame twists the history of U.S. chattel slavery into something that can be rectified in part through increased self-esteem and self-discovery. This formulation of Black pride marks a significant departure from that which was espoused by the Black Power movement. Instead of pride via a reclaimed past, the Black Power movement conceptualized pride through collective struggle that transcended national boundaries; the understanding of pride as shared rather than individual could likewise be seen on the television program *Soul!* (PBS, 1968–73). Featuring an array of Black artists, intellectuals, performers, and public figures performing for an explicitly Black audience, *Soul!* offered a platform for engaging with ideas of cultural nationalism. As Gayle Wald notes, "black culture" on the show was expressly understood as an empowering formation that "countered the historical erasures of white supremacy."[21] Similarly, for the Black Power movement, pride went beyond "merely associating oneself with an idea" to aligning oneself "with a larger struggle."[22] Pride in this iteration thus expresses a form of collective self-making and critique.

Theorizing pride through resistance to white supremacy and the state yielded different goals for the Black Power movement, ones that focused on valorizing the ghetto as a site of pride and power rather than shame. Instead of what Nikhil Singh describes as "the reassuring teleological narrative of black uplift through citizenship," the Black Power movement responded to liberal antiracism's assimilationist approach by calling for anticolonial solidarity.[23] Pride was not solely in the past but in global struggle against colonialism and white supremacy. Marking a distinction between cultural and political pan-Africanism during the era, Singh writes that the "new interest in Africa among U.S. blacks in the 1960s did not simply derive from a psychic quest for positive self-images or genealogical lineages" but rather "such psychic and cultural assertions . . . followed from claims about ethical commonality, global relatedness, and political responsibility."[24] Radical Black activisms critiqued "America's democratic pretensions" and, in so doing, "[severed] their links with the nation."[25]

By contrast, Haley's conception of pride is defined by identity rather than transnational struggle. Haley liberalized the radicalism of the 1960s and the Black Power movement by centering Black pride on the past, and not in histories of maroons and abolitionists. For example, when Sally Reed of *Instructor* magazine asks Haley, "Sociologists claim that the big success of 'Roots' was in terms of what it did for black Americans. What exactly do you think it has done?" Haley's answer is revealing:

Think about the image of Africa everyone grew up with—
both historically and culturally. It was "Jungle Jim." What
"Roots" has done is provide us with a new, better, more
positive image, and, incidently, an incredibly more accurate
image. Up until recently black people were ashamed of their
past. Black people were not proud of slaves shuffling around.
Hopefully "Roots" enabled us to see slaves as heroic—
they survived. That's the most important thing "Roots"
has changed—the image of the black past.[26]

For Haley, *Roots* offers a corrective to racist imagery of Africa and
replaces Black shame with pride and victimhood with survivorship.
This maneuver is echoed in the promotional materials for Miami-
Dade Community College's *Roots* curriculum, which was the most
prolific. According to language arts teacher Ellen Heidt, "My students' awareness of their own roots and the pride associated with
that discovery expanded immeasurably. In place of the image of na-
tives playing drums all day, students learned that whole nations and
races flourished on the African continent. . . . Above all one theme
emerged for each student—Pride. Individual and racial pride acquired new meaning. Rather than hate or resentment, my 'Roots'
project generated a fascinating motivation to learn and feel a heightened self-awareness and self-respect."[27] Crucially, Heidt underscores
that rather than negative emotions—"hate or resentment"—that
might be dangerous to the status quo and white supremacy, her
Roots project increased individual pride and self-esteem, thus working as a form of sentimental education.

In a 1977 interview with the NEA, Haley is asked about whether
it's possible that "Black students won't be able to trace their heritage."
Acknowledging that most "won't be able to trace their roots back to
Africa," Haley states what is most important:

They care enough to go looking at all. This in itself would be a
change from what you and I know to be true: Years ago, Black
people never talked about their slave forebears. We wanted
nothing to do with Africa. If students can go back as far as
their grandparents—and are digging with pride—they are

infinitely better [than] if they were ashamed to go digging at all. It is the spirit of the search that I am concerned with. I want students to say, "I wish I knew more about me," and "I am proud of my ancestors."[28]

The emphasis on pride comprises what Passanante Elman calls an "emotional habitus," which outlines the contours for what is "emotionally possible at a given moment." Particular emotions are constituted as desirable and appropriate, thereby expunging or managing those rendered excessive, inappropriate, or dangerous.[29] In this instance, a pride coupled with genealogical interest in the past dispels other emotions, such as anger at the present. As noted by Miami-Dade Community College, "Those taking the course have gained an appreciation for the strength of our multi-cultural society while obtaining a greater understanding of the values of individual components of our social framework. This new awareness helps to promote positive racial relations."[30] The discourse of multiculturalism and emphasis on understanding—the past, in particular—as the route to "positive" racial relations evinces a conception of race and racism grounded in interpersonal and intercultural difference. Emotions must be managed, aided by sentimental education, in order to appreciate a multicultural understanding of the United States. Further, the emphasis on Black pride evacuates whiteness entirely. There is no mention in the Miami-Dade Community College curricula of white supremacy or even the term *racism*. White shame and culpability are repressed through a focus on putative Black shame about slavery; in the process, whiteness is elided and rendered nonliable.

An entire curriculum centered on the series and pride—"Africa, Roots, and Pride for Afro-Americans"—was developed for an all-Black high school in St. Louis. According to Margaret Campbell, who wrote the teacher's guide to the unit, the TV version of *Roots* provided the majority of her students with "their first positive view of Africa and their own roots." As a result, she emphasized how she will "use this beginning to help foster a sense of pride in my students' African heritage by following Kunta Kinte back to his homeland."[31] Black pride here is figured as a safe one, a shift from the framing of Black pride in the 1960s as "aggressive."[32] By the 1970s, recuperating

supposed Black shame about slavery into pride worked as a lifestyle strategy where Black Americans could have pride in the past
as expressed through contemporary consumer goods: "Mandinka
Maiden" T-shirts, *Roots* music, and genealogy kits.[33] Ad campaigns
during the early 1960s that emphasized racial integration and de-
segregation by the end of the decade morphed into attempts to hail
Black consumers through an emphasis on pride. Unsurprisingly, mar-
keters appropriated Black pride for corporate gain: companies hired
Black consultants to "help themselves 'plug' into the 'soul' scene," and
primers on "Communicating Soul style" promised white readers an
education in the "'vocabulary Soul Brothers Cherish.'"[34] We can thus
see the literal investment in constituting subjects who feel particular
ways in order to support shifting racial formations.

By the time the miniseries aired on ABC in January 1977, the nation's "ethnic revival"—a widespread desire to claim an identity "that
was not simply 'American'"—was in full swing.[35] Increased interest
in the category "ethnicity" was engendered by several factors, including a desire among white people not only to mobilize as ethnic pride
groups (e.g., "Ukrainian Power") akin to Black Power but also to use
ethnicity as a means of exculpation. The focus on "black grievance"
as a national issue prompted a white uptake of ethnicity in order to
disassociate from white privilege. As Matthew Frye Jacobson observes, "The popular rediscovery of ethnic forebears became one
way of saying, 'We're merely newcomers; the nation's crimes are
not our own.'"[36] Claiming one's ethnic identity can thus be read as
a distancing maneuver away from whiteness and culpability. Moreover, the state bestowed recognition and public funding on behalf of
ethnic pluralism, evidenced by the 1972 Ethnic Heritage Studies Act,
which funneled resources to schools and universities in support of
curriculum designed to foster ethnic awareness and identification in
relation to American identity formation. Critically, the authorization
for the act reveals the presumed connection between ethnic history
and domestic harmony: "In a multiethnic society a greater understanding of the contribution of one's own heritage and those of one's
fellow citizens can contribute to a more harmonious, patriotic, and
committed populace."[37] Haley echoed this sentiment in a 1977 interview with the journal *Instructor*. When asked, "What do you think
the pursuit of roots will do for us as a nation?" Haley responded:

It will make us a stronger people if we have a sense of who we are and where we come from. In schools it is very important that while individual students pursue their own family history, it should also be a means to study each other's cultures. The more people know about each other—proud of who they are and where they came from—the less hostility we will have. Hostility is usually born of ignorance.[38]

Pride is constructed as a means toward domestic peace and as a rejoinder to the discourse of Africa as outside of history.[39] According to this logic, reinforcing individual connections to the past results in a strengthened nation bolstered by awareness and tolerance. Yet as Saidiya Hartman demonstrates in *Lose Your Mother*, there is no unmediated access to a pure past. Rather, we choose our inheritances "as much as they are passed on. The past depends less on 'what happened then' than on the desires and discontents of the present."[40] History, in other words, is constituted through the requirements of the present context; for *Roots*, this included the era's antiracist activism.

For the state, quelling and managing domestic disorder and discontent, particularly in the wake of the uprisings of the 1960s, was a continued aim in the 1970s, one that attention to ethnic particularity ostensibly aided. At the same time, the student movements of the 1960s pushed U.S. higher education to open its doors to minoritized students and fields of study, resulting in the emergence of the interdisciplines, including ethnic studies.[41] In other words, activists forced the state, capital, and U.S. academy to respond, and in so doing, each sought to incorporate and make use of minority difference. By adapting to the rise of new figures—women, queer people, people of color—and insurgent epistemologies, power could contain and alter the demands of the era's protest movements. I contend that directing and managing the emotions of citizen-subjects in relation to race and the history of slavery was part of this maneuver—it became necessary to feel a particular version of the past in order to move onward toward colorblindness. The anger of the 1960s and 1970s was redirected toward a melodramatic framing and a curriculum that could reshape it into pride and admiration. *Roots* offered a melodramatic form that could provide a necessary catharsis, one that quelled other responses.

The Gift of Melodrama

The state's investment in minority difference is apparent in the emphasis on racial progress and diversity present in the discourse around the U.S. Bicentennial, the significance of which was not lost on *Roots'* producers. Haley's work was described as a "birthday present" to the United States, something that could help ease the contradictions of a nation founded on slavery and genocide celebrating its birth as a democracy. In a June 1976 *New York Times* article, "A Saga of Slavery That Made the Actors Weep," the series was framed as a "belated Bicentennial gift, a story of true nobility and true horror, an eloquent attempt to find a source of hope in history and ancestry" for viewers able to "accept the premise that 'the hero is the saga'" and who are "willing to follow this family of ordinary Americans from freedom in Juffure in 1750 to a renewal of freedom in Tennessee in 1867." The article quotes producer Stan Margulies about the "theme" of the saga: "'We've come this far. Maybe there's a chance for going further.'"[42] In a 1975 letter from Alex Haley to Margulies, Haley mentions his delight at both the timing and scheduling of the miniseries, noting that he had even been "fantasizing that this could happen, those publication and TV series dates" that represent "the absolute optimum of audience." He continues:

> Even psychologically it's the optimum: after the first eight Bicentennial months, with their flood of this-and-that, including all of the hassles that are sure to result from overcrowded events, and key Bicentennial cities' upset record crowds, finally when with relief the fall arrives, and people are kind of relieved all that's behind, and are settled down back at home, in more or less familiar settings and routines and relaxation, *then* ABC-TV rolls with this magnificent drama. It absolutely cannot be beat for circumstantial brilliant programming.[43]

For Haley, the Bicentennial celebrations primed the *Roots* audience in two ways: by establishing a connection to and interest in early U.S. history and by producing a desire for the relief that television can provide. Using the language of psychology, Haley envisions a move from public crowds to the private and individual space of the home.

The timeline that Haley anticipates—the "first eight Bicentennial months" full of events and crowds, then a return to the routine of the comfortable and the "familiar"—reveals his hope for the possibilities of *Roots* to jolt viewers back into engagement with the unfamiliar, and for a more intimate connection to national history.

The form of the miniseries is significant here. By condensing the narrative over a week rather than several, a miniseries changes television's weekly flow and the affective resonance of a television show airing with several days in between. Typical television programming needs to hold viewer attention over the length of a season. The intent of a miniseries, by contrast, is to arrest viewer attention for the truncated duration of its airing. Temporally, a miniseries is much more fleeting than a series-long television program. If one is fully captivated and immersed for the week, the viewer has successfully engaged the program. In this way, the miniseries form aligns well with the discourse of a quick affective resolution to racism rather than a long, structural one. The miniseries genre is fitting for resolving racism through concentrated feelings instead of the lengthy commitment and imagination required of a structural strategy. This, in turn, aligns with a rising multiculturalism and a consumerist understanding of race framed through the lenses of ethnicity and culture—race is something to be consumed, appreciated, and admired, divorced from material realities.[44] With the emphasis on catharsis leading to admiration, whiteness is rendered innocent.

Through its connection to the Bicentennial, *Roots* became a means to appease contradictions around Black citizenship and slavery—namely, the exclusion of Black people from the category of citizen. Simultaneously, the miniseries offered a way to acknowledge the contradictions while celebrating the Bicentennial and progress. In 1976, Haley criticized Black protest and denial of the Bicentennial celebration, calling it "absolutely ridiculous. . . . We should be aware that there is progress. . . . Only by acknowledging it can we expand on that progress. . . . Obviously we have much, much more to do yet."[45] From the promotional materials to the curricula, the emphasis on progress is central to the story of *Roots*. For instance, the Films Incorporated Teacher's Guide follows the miniseries's teleological understanding of time in its course structure, beginning in Juffure and ending with "freedom" in Tennessee. Although the guide acknowledges the contradictions around Black freedom in the Reconstruction era, wherein the formerly enslaved were subjected to new forms of containment and control—the unit is titled "Emancipated but Not Free"—this is resolved by the final unit, titled "'Hear Me, O African: We Is Free.'"[46]

At the same time, the guide asks students to compare the antebellum era with contemporary political struggles that the guide frames as analogous to chattel slavery. In part five, "Daring to Be Free," the guide instructs teachers to educate students about the Berlin Wall as a "modern restriction on freedom of movement" similar to codes and laws regulating Black movement during the antebellum era. In the first unit, the guide explains that "Millions of people during World War II experienced the same fear and loss of loved ones felt by Kunta and his family. Even today, there is still oppression and inhumanity in our world."[47] The temporal marker "even today" presumes that it might come as a surprise that "oppression and inhumanity" still exist, not yet eradicated by progress. The use of equivalents—comparing slavery to the Holocaust—works to render slavery as not singular but rather a precursor of sorts, one that is frequently minimized in comparison to other atrocities. In the process, specificity is flattened. Rebecca Wanzo contends that this reductive framing yields a binary understanding of "free" and "slave" in relation to liberal citizenship, where the slave is juxtaposed against the free liberal subject.[48] Anti-Black racism is subsumed and located in the past.

Moreover, sentimental education's use of comparison presumes that students need this framework to learn empathy. Teachers are instructed to "ask students to discuss the capture of Jews for extermination" and to point out to students that "atrocities similar to those against Kunta in 1767 and against Jews from 1939 to 1945, are still being committed against South African blacks today." Later in the "Life in America" unit, teachers are guided to have their students "think of modern examples of restrictions on personal movement, both from their own experience (perhaps curfews in urban areas) and from the news (black ghettos in South Africa, the Berlin Wall, etc.)."[49] Eliding and erasing anti-Black racism within the United States is a common maneuver, one that upholds the narrative of progress and antiracist liberalism. Any consideration of the afterlife of slavery and contemporary anti-Black racism is studiously avoided; through a focus on elsewhere, the unit erases U.S.-based racial struggle. Further, the relationship between equivalence and sentimentality underscores the mainstream invisibility of Black suffering and whiteness's willful inability to see Black pain. In order to teach students how to empathize with Kunta Kinte, the guides rely on what Wanzo calls the "homogenization of suffering," thereby erasing important distinctions and the ways that anti-Blackness renders Black suffering an oxymoron.[50] As Hartman explains, Black suffering is so hard to see because of a racist optics rooted in slavery.[51] Comparativity asks for a transfer of feeling from one minoritized group to another, a move that Alexander Weheliye suggests is pointless in the face of the enduring calculus of race that continues to render individuals and populations disposable. This disposability exposes racialized populations "to different forms of political violence on a daily basis," and as such, "it seems futile to tabulate, measure, or calculate their/our suffering in the jargon of comparison."[52]

When present-day African American communities are acknowledged in the lesson plan, it is reminiscent of the culture of poverty thesis described in chapter 1. According to this discourse, poverty is an issue of lifestyle and values rather than economic inequality and structural barriers rooted in white supremacy and heteropatriarchy. As a possible research project for Unit 7, the guide suggests having students "compare the family structure of traditional African society with that of black families living in America today." Students are asked to "1. Suggest how the structures are similar; 2. Indicate which of the structures is more matriarchal; 3. Discuss the universal importance of the family unit in the socialization process."[53] In an earlier unit, suggestions for more extensive projects ask students to ponder the following questions:

Consider the effect of the frequent separations experienced by slaves on their concept of the family. Were slaves allowed to marry a spouse of their choice? How frequently were families separated? *Is the black family structure today different than the white family structure?* Do you think black slaves were bonded together more closely because of their shared pain,

or were they afraid to make personal commitments because
their futures were always uncertain? Does the inability to
control your destiny breed fatalism?[54]

This is reminiscent of the liberal pathologization of the Black family
discussed in chapter 1, where the figure of the Black matriarch is held
responsible for the devastations of slavery. The Moynihan Report
thus helped to shape the sentimental regard for slavery by constituting subjects to be pitied (Black men who are oppressed by matriar-
chy) but who also suffer from fatalism where instead they should take
personal responsibility. The guide articulates this in terms of feelings: slaves were "afraid to make personal commitments." This uptake of the Moynihan Report shifts the focus from white supremacy
to a need to feel differently: less entitled, more responsible. According to this logic, slavery taught Black people to fear commitment,
and this is offered as an explanation for the "difference" of Black
family structures from white ones. The curricula suggest that Black
people are plagued by the emotions of slavery—not fear of white supremacist terror or internalized racism but, rather, shame requiring
a hero. Using the ravages of slavery to "explain" Black families, the
teacher's guide echoes the Moynihan Report, particularly when it
asks students how family structures are different along a Black/white
divide. The first option, if Black communities were constituted and
strengthened through shared grief, is negated by the "or," suggesting
the correct answer for students to choose.

   Angela Davis offers a strong counterpoint to this negation. In her
1971 essay "Reflections on the Black Woman's Role in the Community of Slaves," Davis critiques the Moynihan Report's degradation
of Black women and disrupts the myth of the Black matriarch. Davis
provides a Black feminist rejoinder to the racialized misogyny of the
Moynihan Report and, implicitly, Haley's masculinist narrative of a
male hero. She writes, "The image of black women enchaining their
men, cultivating relationships with the oppressor, is a cruel fabrica-
tion," one that serves "to impair our capacity for resistance today by
foisting upon us the ideal of male supremacy."[55] By contrast, Davis
describes the profound courage of Black women resisting and surviv-
ing slavery and the role that women played in making survival possible for others. Tracing the multiple and varied ways that enslaved

women challenged slavery, Davis argues that "the contributions of strong black women" took place within a "community of resistance."[56] Women posed a unique threat to slavery because, as Davis identifies, women had access to the only sphere over which the enslaver did not have total control: the slave household.[57] As such, the quotidian oppression of Black women "had to assume an unconcealed dimension of outright counter-insurgency."[58] This counterinsurgency took the form of the enslaver's rape and sexual domination of Black women as a terroristic means to "destroy her proclivities towards resistance."[59] Rape functioned as a way for the enslaver to reproduce the slave economy and, as Davis argues, guard against the possible revolutions or rebellions that the Black woman might incite given her access to a space not utterly controlled by the enslaver. Roots' narrative focus on a singular male hero, which occludes what Davis identifies as the Black woman's central role in fomenting rebellion, aligns with Haley's liberal progress narrative, which obscures the possibility of contemporary rebellion. The patriarchal narrative of slavery via the figure of Kunta Kinte is particularly significant in the face of Margaret Walker's charge of plagiarism against Haley. Her 1966 novel Jubilee narrates the history of slavery through a woman, Vyry Brown, and in 1977, Walker sued Haley for plagiarism, claiming that "fifteen scenes from Jubilee showed up in Roots."[60] While Haley's masculinist narrative garnered widespread success, Walker's was obscured.

Similarly, in 1959, Lorraine Hansberry was commissioned by NBC to write a script for one of what was intended to be a series of ninety-minute television dramas in commemoration of the Civil War Centennial. Hansberry wrote The Drinking Gourd, a piece depicting the change in power on enslaver Hiram Sweet's plantation on the eve of the Civil War. In the work, Rissa, mother to Hannibal and Isaiah, is enslaved by the elderly and infirm Hiram Sweet, whose adult son Everett is eager to modernize plantation management by hiring poor white people (embodied by a character named Zeb) as overseers. Hiram disagrees with Everett's desires to increase production through intensified violence and exploitation, and demonstrates guilt (and feigns innocence) when he later visits Rissa in her cabin after learning that Everett ordered Zeb to blind Hannibal upon discovering that he could read and write. The script, which was deemed "too controversial" for a mainstream television audience and thus never produced, ends with Rissa delivering Hiram's gun to Hannibal and two others seeking escape to see them off into the night.[61] *The Drinking Gourd* was, as Imani Perry writes in her biography of Hansberry, "far from a simplistic demonization of white Southerners," which may have been more palatable to network executives.[62] As written, *The Drinking Gourd* was considered by skittish executives to be too much of a "hot potato," according to Robert Nemiroff, in part due to its complex representation of the totalizing and systematic nature of U.S. chattel slavery.[63]

Indeed, as Nemiroff wrote in his analysis about why the script was rejected, it was precisely because Hansberry crafted an intricate portrayal of slavery's devastations rather than a reductive melodrama with clear moral divisions:

> It was not even the horrors she showed—the fact that the young black hero was to be shown on perhaps fifty million American home screens being blinded for the statutory crime of learning to read—but the fact that she insisted upon empathizing as well with the *white* forced to blind him! In a medium not noted for the avoidance of horror, an industry whose stock-in-trade is violence, one might suppose that this image could be tolerated. But the approach to Zeb Dudley and Hiram Sweet was something else again.[64]

Hansberry's work was about systems and structures rather than individuals; according to Nemiroff, Hansberry sought not "guilt but action."[65] In contrast to Alex Haley's triumphant narrative that ultimately affirmed rather than critiqued capitalism, Hansberry's *The Drinking Gourd* considers slavery as the foundation of U.S. economic philosophy.[66] The screenplay begins with the commodity—in this case, cotton—as the script's narrator, "The Soldier," feels the materiality of the earth and remarks upon the centrality of this crop to slavery.[67] Hansberry explicitly connects the commodity to slavery and specifically the racialized system that demanded the transformation of a human being into a commodity. In her attention to systems, Hansberry highlights the strategy of "divide and conquer" along racial lines, yet does not subsume class under race. Through the character Zeb, an impoverished white man considering moving west to improve his family's lot, Hansberry shows "how class and social stratification among whites sustained slavery and maintained investment in it, even though poor whites were more victimized by economic exploitation than they were beneficiaries of whiteness."[68] When Hiram's son Everett approaches Zeb to ask if he would work on the plantation as the new overseer, a preacher who is in Zeb's home reproaches him, explaining that the ownership class does not care about poor white people and in fact openly derides them. Undeterred, Zeb returns to the promise of the wages of whiteness and white masculinity in particular: "I'm a white man, Preacher! And I'm goin' to drive slaves for Everett Sweet and he's goin' to pay me for it and this time next year, Zeb Dudley aims to own himself some slaves and be a man—you hear!"[69] Throughout the script, Hansberry deftly points to the production of gender through slavery, including white femininity. Although Hansberry's script does not focus heavily on Hiram's wife, Maria, it is clear in a scene from act 2 that she is more fervent than Hiram about intensifying labor and violence on the plantation in the service of increasing capital. When she discovers Hiram talking with Rissa about how he will not put Hannibal in the field, Rissa "sees Maria and becomes quite still. Hiram follows her eyes and turns to see Maria as she advances toward him with the medicine and water, her face set in silent anger."[70] Hansberry makes clear that white femininity is likewise implicated in chattel slavery despite claims to racial innocence.

Whereas Alex Haley and *Roots* producer David Wolper "welcomed and encouraged" a response to *Roots* as a "'universal' family story," Hansberry's depiction of family in *The Drinking Gourd* is not about a masculinist arc of progress, nor is it a universalist narrative of triumph.[71] Rather, through Everett's insistence on taking over management of the plantation and his ongoing faith in the South to prevail (despite his father's fears about how a war would turn out), the reader sees how the legacies of whiteness are transferred generationally and adaptive to the demands of racial capitalism, the "system that *required* the crimes."[72] In act 1's argument between Hiram and Everett, the doctor visiting an ailing Hiram sides with the former: "You and I have to face the fact that this is a new era, Hiram. Cotton is a big business in a way it never was before. If you treat it any other way, you're lost. You just have to adjust to that, Hiram. For the good of yourself and for the good of the South."[73] Hiram is cast as one of a dying breed, yet he can be assured that whiteness (and whiteness as property) will be transferred through his patriarchal lineage and legacy.[74]

Feeling Slavery

Roots' melodramatic form provided an accessible framework through which sentimental education could shape the contours of appropriate feeling in relation to slavery. Moreover, as Rebecca Wanzo suggests, the representation of slavery works as an especially "powerful referent in U.S sentimental political storytelling because it epitomizes suffering sanctioned and then acknowledged as a grave wrong by the state; thus it exemplifies the possibility of state shame and subsequent state action."[75] For *Roots*, however, state shame is renarrated as Black shame about the past, now recuperated through a male hero and a depoliticized Black pride. Melodrama offers what Linda Williams suggests is the key form through which U.S. popular culture has discussed and understood race—namely, framing it as a "moral dilemma."[76] Relying on a dualistic logic of good versus evil, victim versus villain, melodrama thus "recognizes virtue, expresses the inexpressible, and reconciles the irreconcilables of American culture."[77] Racial melodrama, and sentimentality more broadly, has long been used as a means toward rights and liberal inclusion by gaining the "moral upper hand" through a depiction of racialized and gendered suffering.[78] Put another way, melodrama as a mode for framing (and constructing) Black/white race relations relies on the successful deployment of emotion, with the anticipated catharsis at the end. The catharsis signals a completion, marked by the relief of feeling and releasing strong emotions. It is precisely the act of feeling that is central to melodrama. By working hard to teach feeling, the *Roots* curricula imply that the melodramatic form alone is not sufficient to establish the proper emotions for a new racial epoch in which citizen-subjects must align their feelings and behaviors with the official antiracism espoused by the state and capital.

Although racial melodrama shares similarities to the "damage imagery" used by social scientists discussed in chapter 1, given the presumption that moral legitimacy and sympathy are powerful, these tactics work differently via distinct cultural forms. Melodrama privileges emotions and the emotional production itself is the end goal. Further, melodrama's ability to simplify complex social and political issues readily lends itself to pedagogy. Beyond moral instruction, melodramas "provide emotional scenarios that act as lessons on proper political feelings."[79] By contrast, "damage imagery" is a pathologizing social scientific discourse reliant on claims to neutrality and objectivity. Emotions are not the end point but rather are deployed toward other goals, such as policy changes. Crucially, Saidiya Hartman's reading of *Uncle Tom's Cabin* does not presume white sympathy but instead emphasizes white pleasure at Black suffering; if empathy is present, it serves to recenter whiteness and erase the enslaved.[80] By feeling sadness via the *Roots* melodrama, white viewers align with a constitution of whiteness as sympathetic toward Blackness. Describing the asymmetrical power relations of empathy, Sara Ahmed notes that this results in "an appropriation that transforms and perhaps even neutralizes their pain into our sadness."[81] Further, the process whereby viewers and students learn feeling through melodrama is a normativizing one—some lives are constituted as grievable, worthy of mourning, and deserving of empathy and others are not.[82]

Teaching Feeling

The melodramatic form of *Roots* was central to its appeal as a pedagogical tool. In a memo from Miami-Dade Community College president Robert McCabe to academic institutions interested in the *Roots* course, McCabe reassures teachers anxious about the miniseries (rather than week-by-week) scheduling, noting that the week of *Roots* "will touch virtually every family in America, and these gripping dramatic presentations should leave millions of Americans with a desire to learn more. . . . From the academic standpoint, the dramatic telecasts have always been thought of as *contributing in the affective domain* and in motivating for further study. There is a feeling among the staff that the presentation of the full series in eight days will produce maximum impact."[83] Similar to Haley's excitement over the series' timing, the contribution to the "affective domain" is heightened by the miniseries format, which condenses and heightens feeling to a week. The emotional impact of the series was highlighted in teacher's guides as well. As one guide notes, although the program "is in no way intended as a substitute for lectures" and the television characters should motivate students to engage with print materials, "the series provides an affective impact beyond anything any of us could as individual teachers."[84] The "Teacher's Guide to Roots for Elementary Grades" in particular spends a significant amount of pedagogical energy on guiding teachers in how students should feel. For example, in "The Passage to America" unit, the guide emphasizes, "The journey to America was unquestionably the most traumatic and humiliating of all slave experiences. When your students begin to learn about it, they will feel justifiably outraged at the inhumanity of the slave system and understandably proud of the course of those slaves who somehow managed to survive."[85] The guide then offers facts to help explain the "hardships" endured by Kunta Kinte. Students will feel "outraged" and "proud" when learning about the Middle Passage—no other feelings are presented as options. Outrage and pride are thus shored up as the proper emotions to feel, although the outrage is one that is contained to the "inhumanity of the slave system," not white supremacy or slavery's afterlife. The affective production of outrage and pride diverts attention from structural racism.

Even the program's effectiveness was measured in feelings. Miami-Dade Community College surveyed students taking its *Roots* course and compiled the findings in a report titled "What Do Students Say about the Television Series on Roots?" The survey questions, focused primarily on feelings, included, "How would you say the TV series on *Roots* affected you in terms of your feelings about yourself and your ancestry?"; "How would you say the TV series on *Roots* affected you in terms of your feelings about Americans that do not share your cultural heritage?"; and "How would you say the TV Series on *Roots* affected you in terms of your feelings about American history?"[86] As a result, the responses were framed in terms of feelings: "I feel ashamed that any of my ancestors could have done such a thing to human beings"; "Hopefully that is behind us and this series will enlighten me in my understanding of others." Importantly, in response to the question about personal ancestry, the highest number of survey respondents indicated that the series "Aroused my interest and curiosity about my ancestry/stimulated me to trace my ancestry/made me realize that tracing one's ancestry can make a person a better person/wished my relatives were around to tell me about my ancestry/made me appreciate my families which have preserved our culture." Coming in second were the responses indicating shame and guilt: "Made me feel ashamed of my ancestry, how cruel and inhuman they were/fortunately, my ancestors did not own slaves/I'm glad I did not belong to that generation of whites/wonder whether my ancestors treated blacks like that." (Twenty-seven respondents also said, "Did not affect me in any way.")[87]

Focusing on individual feelings and disconnecting them from structural issues, the survey avoids the political possibilities of emotion—the power of affect and sentimental storytelling can, of course, be significant political tools with the capacity to engender institutional change. Although emotions are often separated from politics, Wanzo considers how emotions can be motivational, a "necessary prerequisite to social and political action."[88] Most viewers had deep feelings about *Roots* that could have been a foundation for collective political struggle rather than merely heightened individual self-awareness. Yet for *Roots*, sentiment and emotions are harnessed for a different end: not structural change but instead a change of heart requiring nothing else. This is especially evident in the surge of genealogical research following the January 1977 broadcast. According to Jacobson, "Hundreds of thousands of white Americans descended on local libraries and archives in search of information, not about slavery or black history, but about themselves and their own ethnic past."[89] The curricula based on *Roots* took this up as well, focusing on projects like creating one's family tree.

In this case, an emphasis on emotions prevents attention to structural racism and the concerted effort by neoconservatives during the 1970s to erode the limited gains of the civil rights movement. By the time the decade began, a neoliberal logic of "empowerment" was taking hold as part of the right-wing backlash against entitlement programs, thereby blaming the poor for their own poverty.[90] A confluence of factors during this era resulted in increased levels of Black poverty and segregation, perhaps none more so than white flight en masse to the suburbs—augmented by racist housing policies and federal support—that left cities economically devastated by the loss of property tax revenue. Between 1960 and 1977, "four million whites moved out of central cities . . . while the number of whites living in suburbs increased by 22 million."[91]

According to historian David Freund, white people viewed these
all-white suburbs as "sanctuaries" from urban Black life, particularly
the urban uprisings of the 1960s in cities like Detroit, Newark, and
Los Angeles.[92] White people in northern cities and suburbs inter-
preted Black resistance to white supremacy as "confirmation that
black people posed a threat to their families, their economic well-
being, and their 'way of life'—all of which were increasingly tied up
in whites' status as property owners." By the 1960s, white people
grasped a new vocabulary that enabled them to claim antiracism
while simultaneously opposing civil rights reform.[93] In addition to
white flight, George Lipsitz describes how urban renewal between
the 1930s and the 1970s systematically destroyed approximately 1,600
Black neighborhoods in cities throughout the country, resulting in
an incalculable "financial and emotional cost on black communities."[94] Black displacement continued into the 1970s and, despite
claims to the contrary, urban renewal actually demolished rather
than increased low-income housing. As Douglas Massey and Nancy
Denton demonstrate, white people bolstered systematic exclusion
with harassment and violence, continuously resisting any attempt
at integration. When Black entry was successful, subsequent white
homeseekers ensured resegregation by avoiding the neighborhood;
existing white homeowners fled to the suburbs.[95] By the end of the
decade, unemployment had reached record levels, along with "in-
flation, falling wages, increasing income inequality, and rising rates
of Black poverty. Not only did the ghetto fail to disappear; in many
ways, its problems multiplied."[96]

At the same time, economic restructuring beginning in the 1970s
further concentrated poverty and entrenched racial segregation, as
deindustrialization left U.S. cities decimated. Despite the fact that
neoliberal restructuring and neoconservative efforts to gut the welfare
state are general social problems, Lipsitz contends that the "possessive investment in whiteness" uses race to blame racialized populations for the state's overall disinvestment. People of color are thereby
constructed as failures while whiteness is rendered innocent.[97] In Lipsitz's theorization of whiteness, he centers the monetary value that
accrues to whiteness via advantages gained through racial discrimination in education, health, housing, and labor. Similarly, Cheryl
Harris argues that whiteness is constituted as a crucial property and

valuable inheritance in part through its exclusivity and exclusion. To maintain its value, whiteness must be founded on what it is not (and who is excluded); as white people receive more rights, Black people receive fewer in a never-ending cycle of oppression where white life and white rights are based on Black subjugation.[98] The racialized transfer of wealth in the United States relies on the state to play a key role in promoting and maintaining white accumulation through the racialization of citizenship, economic status, and all aspects of social life. The sedimentation of racial inequality is a result of cumulative wealth accrued through generations of state support for white wealth and Black poverty. Due to a multitude of factors, including neoliberal restructuring and the continuous undermining of civil rights gains, Black college enrollments and completion rates declined since 1976, "threatening to wipe out the gains of the 1960s and 1970s."[99] The advances of the civil rights movement began to wane and the "condition of the most disadvantaged African Americans deteriorated rapidly after 1970" even as the middle class grew.[100]

By emphasizing emotions and catharsis rather than attending to larger structures, Miami-Dade Community College, Films Incorporated, and Wolper Productions ignored the larger context impending on *Roots*. Whiteness (and the investment in it) is reproduced "in new form in every era"—that is, racism and white supremacy are flexible and adaptive.[101] In relation to *Roots*, whiteness is bound up with feeling differently to the detriment of broader structural responses.[102] The sentimental education of *Roots* and the supplemental educational material aligned with the changes to racism and white supremacy wrought by the emergence of official antiracism and the work of activists.

White Comfort

Critics of the book's adaptation to the television miniseries argue that producer fears about alienating white TV viewers informed creative decisions, resulting in a whitewashed version of Haley's story. For instance, Brandon Stoddard, then head of ABC's novels for television, emphasized the need to cast familiar white actors for the comfort of white viewers.[103] In a later letter from Wolper to Stoddard regarding a *Roots* rerun, Wolper references the decision:

I think that there should be more white people in some of
the commercials for the show. We casted white comfortable
television stars; which I believe was one of the reasons for it
being successful, and I think they should be in some of the
spots you show as you get closer to the air date.[104]

By casting familiar white actors, critics argued, the white characters
were more relatable and less likely to produce white discomfort.
This happened at the level of characterization as well, with Captain
Davies portrayed as an upstanding, religious man who merely got
caught up in the slave trade. As a result, the "inhumanity of [first
mate Slater], and of the institution of slavery itself, is made more
palatable by the humanity of Davies."[105] According to William Blinn,
head writer for the miniseries, "For our purposes, [Davies] was certainly not a sympathetic man. An understandable man, yes—but it
is clearly absurd to have a likeable slaveship captain. It was equally
unwise, we thought, to do four hours of television without showing
a white person with whom we could identify."[106] The producers were
aware that rationalizations like Blinn's were grounds for critique,
along with the lack of Black directors, producers, or scriptwriters involved in the production. In a 1976 memo, Margulies explains how
to respond to those arguing that *Roots* was being told from a white
perspective: "The point is: we are not telling Black history from 'our
point of view'—we are presenting Alex Haley's point of view."[107] A
"suggested viewer advisory" from October 1976 similarly anticipated
critiques of sanitizing history: "What you are about to see is a recrea-
tion of a segment of the past. It is authentic as years of research can
make it. It is harsh; as harsh as the world it depicts. It has not been
sensationalized nor has it been sterilized."[108] It is unsurprising that
the transformation of the literary to the visual *Roots* was accompanied by sanitization. Yet this maneuver is significant for what it reveals about producer anxieties about affect and the potential power
of *Roots*.

In March 1976, ABC's Department of Broadcast Standards and
Practices compiled a four-page report of revisions to the script and
production. Of "particular concern" to the department was the "sexual victimization of slave women by their captors," due partly to standards around nudity and sexual content on network television. (The

department took a similar stance with the auction scene, noting that "all slaves are to be clothed" and that any emphasis "placed on the slave's sexual attributes by the AUCTIONEER" are "unacceptable."[109]) Predictably, the libidinal economy of slavery is thus expunged in order to cleanse history for commercial television, but the report connects this erasure to the management of emotion. It continues:

> The sexual victimization of the women must be portrayed but not pounded into the viewer to the point where *his emotional reaction becomes so great* that the above mentioned modifiers are no longer sufficient to support his willingness to receive the program in the spirit in which it is intended.[110]

To resolve this problem, they urge a deletion of scenes—namely, where enslaved women are attacked. Further, "The scene between FANTA and CAPT. DAVIES on pages 107–108, scenes 362–265 must be modified to relieve, for a moment, the pervasive sense of sexual degradation that is present throughout most of the film."[111] This paragraph is rich for what it divulges about how ABC viewed the project. In order to be authentic and historically accurate, the production must include sexual violence, yet it should be done in such a way that the imagined male viewer (women are not even considered) does not stop watching due to being emotionally overwhelmed. Emotions like anger, grief, guilt, and shame need to be contained. We can thus see the careful management of affect based on aesthetics and visual choices, including the suppression of key scenes from Haley's book. The focus on relief emphasizes the containment of emotional reaction to certain parameters.

Moreover, the obscuring of the relationship between rape and slavery perpetuates the erasure of Black women's roles in the slave economy. Enslaved women were particularly vulnerable to sexual violence in an economy based on institutionalized rape.[112] As Black feminists have demonstrated, Black women under slavery were "simply instruments guaranteeing the growth of the slave labor force. They were 'breeders'—animals, whose monetary value could be precisely calculated in terms of their ability to multiply their numbers."[113] Rape additionally functioned as a tool of terror and, as Angela Davis notes, a means for white enslavers to quell insurrection incited by

Black women. The affective management of rape and sexual violence in the televisual *Roots* works to both minimize Black women and control the political possibilities of emotion.

Along these lines, the Department of Broadcast Standards had related issues about different types of violence and brutality, namely whether or not the "maximum tolerance of our audience for violent action" would be pushed beyond what they deemed acceptable. ABC wanted to avoid a "visceral assault upon the viewing audience." In addition to not "assaulting" the audience, ABC feared inciting certain members of it, as the memo made clear:

> We have one further point regarding the language in the film. The effect of this program should be to enrich our sense of history and the perspective of American race relations. Elements of the script that could be interpreted as inflammatory metaphors for contemporary conditions should not be stressed.[114]

ABC viewed the project as one that highlighted slavery in ways that established it as safely in the past. *Roots* would supplement existing U.S. history and contextualize "American race relations," understood as Black and white, in a manner that did not inflame the audience by drawing attention to the present moment as meaning anything but progress from the antebellum era. The memo continues, "For example, lines such as Kunta's 'Kill the white man,' should be treated with an awareness of their potential effect in our modern context."[115] Without insisting upon deletion, the Department of Broadcast Standards made clear that connecting the legacy of slavery to contemporary everyday life through Black militancy was a risk that ABC was not willing to take; instead, the present and the past must be effectively severed. ABC thus worked to manage (Black) conduct by editing the language of the text and by erasing Black women, while simultaneously attempting to protect white audiences from feeling complicit. White audiences were thus shielded from difficult feelings, any sense of responsibility, and confrontation from Black people.

Margulies was similarly concerned about overwhelming the audience. Writing to Stoddard in May 1976, Margulies explains that a scene with "the Redd Foxx character" occurs "at the wrong place and with the wrong actors." He continues:

> Bill and I both feel that it should *not* be played at the auction because it would immediately be followed by the sale of Fanta and then the sale of Kunta—and three consecutive tear-jerkers are probably one more than an audience can accept in a brief time span. Secondly, the scene is played by two characters new to the audience: Fiddler and the Foxx character.[116]

Concerns about maintaining audience attention are certainly not unusual for television production. In the case of *Roots*, however, which the producers continually claimed and presented as "authentic" and "historically accurate," a fixation on comforting white viewers and managing audience emotion works to circumscribe the history of U.S. chattel slavery. Although an early press release described the series as the "emotionally shattering and historically unprecedented saga of the genesis of an American family," the producers were careful to remain within liberal boundaries acceptable to a mainstream white audience.[117]

As LeVar Burton stated in the Family Channel's 1992 promotion of the re-airing of *Roots*, a new generation of people will benefit from exposure to the miniseries:

> It continues to be not only a piece of excellent television, but a powerful teaching tool and a powerful tool of understanding and enlightenment. It's essential that every generation of Americans have the opportunity *to feel the feelings that the experience of watching 'Roots' brings up for us.* In that way, it becomes a powerful healing tool.[118]

Just as the television documentaries were understood as an enlightening technology, here, too, television is figured as a means for racial enlightenment. According to a Miami-Dade Community College brochure about *Roots*, "The reaction to the book and television series,

'Roots,' continues to prod the American people into new understandings and directions. The 'Roots' phenomena resulted in the great-
est awareness concerning the history of Black Americans since the
birth of our nation."[119] Racism and the legacies of slavery are thus addressed through feeling and experiencing emotional catharsis, aided
by curricular materials highlighting the significance of sentimental
education. In so doing, *Roots* has nothing to say about the devastating
material effects of whiteness and the afterlife of slavery. The circular
nature of temporality and race, wherein white supremacy modifies
and adapts over time, is evident in Burton's February 2016 comment
in press releases announcing the trailer for the 2016 *Roots* remake, for
which he is a coexecutive producer.[120] Echoing his quotation from
1992, Burton states, "Nearly 40 years ago I had the privilege to be a part
of an epic television event that started an important conversation in
America. I am incredibly proud to be a part of this new retelling and
start the dialogue again, at a time when it is needed more than ever."[121]
The affective management present throughout the curricula and discourse around *Roots* is crucial to shifting the United States toward a
postracial, liberal, multicultural future. In the wake of Ferguson and
with the rise of Black Lives Matter, *Roots* is offered once again as a
means toward healing in the name of the status quo.

CHAPTER 3

Choosing Freedom

Empathy and Agency

*I'm calling for investments in educational technology that
will help create . . . educational software that's as compelling
as the best video game. I want you guys to be stuck on a video
game that's teaching you something other than just blowing
something up.*

—Barack Obama, March 2011

As the previous two chapters illustrate, shifting racial formations within the *longue durée* of the post–civil rights era were
enmeshed with affective governance and the cultivation of particular feelings. This emotional management served to contain and
discipline the potential threat of more unruly emotions—namely
rage, particularly when racialized as Black—from further disrupting the status quo. Moreover, the catharsis promised by *Roots*, part
of a broader embrace of "ethnicity" and multiculturalism during the
1970s, laid the groundwork for the discourse of colorblindness and
an imagined postracial future. In this chapter, I turn to the emotions
undergirding this shift to neoliberal multiculturalism to suggest
that within this formation, whiteness is constituted in part through
empathizing with a racialized other. In the realm of pedagogy, such
empathy is ostensibly produced through the media form promising
interactivity and immersion: an educational video game (edugame).

On January 24, 2012, the PBS station THIRTEEN released *Mission 2: Flight to Freedom*, a role-playing edugame about U.S. chattel
slavery and the second in the *Mission US* series of edugames designed
to teach U.S. history to middle school students.[1] Timed to coincide
with Black History Month, the release of *Flight to Freedom* occurred

thirty-five years to the day after the initial airing of *Roots* on January 24, 1977. As a member of WNET (formerly the Educational Broadcasting Corporation) in New York, THIRTEEN collaborated with historians to develop the game's content, including scholars from the American Social History Project/Center for Media and Learning at CUNY, and received a $3.3 million grant from the Corporation for Public Broadcasting to create the game.[2] According to promotional materials for *Mission US*, the game immerses students in "rich historical settings" where they are then "empowered . . . to make choices that illuminate how ordinary people experienced the past."[3] In *Flight to Freedom*, players inhabit the character Lucy, a fourteen-year-old girl enslaved in 1848, two years before the passage of the Fugitive Slave Act. Set in northern Kentucky and southern Ohio, the game begins with Lucy on the King plantation outside Lexington. Divided into five parts plus prologue and epilogue, the game requires students to navigate choices provided in order to help Lucy "find a path to freedom."[4] *Flight to Freedom* is part of a larger curriculum with an interactive website featuring teacher's guides, activities, and primary source documents that, promotional materials claim, "show the broader social, political, and economic context of events and perspectives featured in the game."[5]

The racialized relationship of empathy for the enslaved through immersion—according to the game's discourse, one "becomes" a slave through playing the game—is central to racialized governance and, in particular, works to distance whiteness from racism. Although empathy has a longer temporality than a catharsis spurred by racial melodrama, its production through the game similarly constitutes an emotional solution to grappling with the history and afterlife of U.S. chattel slavery. The game's discursive positioning as civic instruction adds another dimension, especially through its emphasis on agency as a recuperative means to entering U.S. history. In *Flight to Freedom*, the Black body is not passive or wounded but agential. Moreover, agency here also provides access to the category "human." As the promotional materials note, the game's explicit intent is to frame resistance as small, quotidian choices, aiming "to humanize enslaved people and present them with dignity, courage, fear, and real human emotions like love and hate. The mission portrays enslaved African Americans with agency and personal power (even when social, economic, and political power was non-existent), and as central actors in their own destinies. Our goal is for all students to develop a greater respect for African Americans' struggle and African American history as a part of American history."[6] In this way, *Flight to Freedom* takes up the project of *Roots*—incorporating African American history into U.S. history overall, encouraging admiration for African American struggle—through the medium of the video game. *Flight to Freedom* suggests that there are ideal ways of being and behaving—namely, through action—thereby reproducing the notion that a liberal actor is the universal subject of history.[7] The emphasis on Black agency modifies the discourse around *Roots* to stress choice. *Flight to Freedom* does not punish but rather seeks to include, particularly in the realm of agency. According to a press release, *Flight to Freedom* "helps students learn how enslaved people's choices—from small, everyday acts of resistance to action that sought an end to slavery—affected the lives of individuals, and ultimately the nation." Enslaved people are "central actors in their own destinies."[8]

The connection between these affective experiences—empathy and agency—becomes evident when attending to temporality and historical context. The rise of neoliberal colorblindness and postrace as a formation, wherein ideal neoliberal citizen-subjects deny the centrality of race to everyday life, is in some ways a residual one with respect to an emerging wokeness. Yet the emphasis on agency is ensconced in a neoliberal understanding of empowerment, thereby erasing historical and current systemic racism. Racial empathy and the supposed gift of freedom—this inclusion into agency under neoliberal multiculturalism and a postrace future—expunges how the agency of the liberal subject required the denial of Black agency.[9] This articulation of empathy, in turn, disavows contemporary racism. In other words, in the context of neoliberal multiculturalism, an amalgam of discourses of colorblindness, choice, and agency coalesce to produce a racial formation where whiteness is distanced from racism through empathy. Official antiracism under neoliberalism requires the production of empathetic subjects who should understand and promote the self as not racist.

Flight to Freedom's emphasis on choice and agency works alongside instruction in feeling, with the presumption that students will gain a better understanding of life as an enslaved person, thereby leading to more empathy. Empathy, agency, admiration, and choice entangle here in the production of feeling, helping to constitute norms and feelings of national belonging. If, as Aubrey Anable suggests, games provide us an opportunity to rehearse feelings, *Flight to Freedom* allows its players to try on empathy for a racialized other.[10] Critically, the game format and its claims to immersion underscore the exigencies of the current media landscape, with the digital offering an interactive way to engage with the history of slavery and supposed immersion to feel.

Whereas 1960s documentaries were addressed to white audiences and taught white viewers to eradicate "prejudice," *Flight to Freedom* does not acknowledge racism at all. This modification of neoliberal colorblindness emphasizes Blackness as agential while obscuring the fact that white people were the instigators and beneficiaries of slavery. In other words, *Flight to Freedom* avoids any theorization of race that centers white supremacy (or even racism). The only mention of "racism" in the entire 322-page "Complete *Flight to Freedom* Classroom Guide" is in reference to *Roots*, which is listed as an additional media resource and described as concluding with a "freed slave who battles against racism in the post-bellum South."[11] Neither *race* nor *racism* are included in the glossary of key terms for the game. The absence of racism or a critical discussion of whiteness teaches students a very safe kind of resistance and agency for the status quo, one that does not challenge white supremacy.

Mission US, Public Media, and Games

Although *Flight to Freedom* has faced outcry for gamifying slavery, the game's creators—the bulk of whom come from THIRTEEN— draw on the association with PBS to enhance the game's credibility and educational value, characterizing it as a form of serious media. The creators of *Flight to Freedom* have defended the game from critics who claim that it minimizes and whitewashes the history of slavery by highlighting the credentials of the scholars involved in the project, including Christopher Moore, a historian and former curator at the Schomburg Center for Research in Black Culture.[12] As one critic notes, the game reduces the complexities of slavery to poor choices on the part of slaves: "Yes, Lucy, you'll get a beating, and it's not because you are a slave who is owned by an evil slave owner, but because you chose the wrong path. Thus, consequences."[13] In response, WNET Education declared publicly that they "stand by [the game]" and that *Flight to Freedom* does not differ from history books unable to "cover all the ills of slavery" even as it "tells some ugly truths about slavery."[14]

With more than three million registered *Mission US* users, the game and its sponsors and partners continue PBS's discursive linkage between public media and citizenship. This is evident in the game's positioning as one solution to what the American History and Civics Initiative—a project funded by the Corporation for Public Broadcasting—identified as "critical shortfalls in middle and high school students' knowledge of American history, our political system, and their roles as citizens."[15] *Mission US* and other supplementary activities by PBS are residual examples of public media's founding mission to enlighten a culturally impoverished public and to manage unrest in the wake of the social movements of the 1960s and 1970s. After the passage of the 1967 Public Broadcasting Act, the Public Broadcasting System (PBS) was established in 1969 as a tool "to address angry, marginalized, and disenfranchised populations," one able to "mediate conflicts, restore liberal pluralism, and facilitate social order."[16] Further, public television had an expressly civic function and impetus to guide, manage, and discipline the middlebrow into "the taste culture from which [PBS] sprang"—that of the elite.[17] Offered as a corrective to the "vast wasteland" of commercial television, PBS worked to constitute citizens versed in the high arts of classical music, great literature, serious documentaries, and gourmet cooking. Quality television, characterized by elite tastes masked as universal, would cultivate quality citizens by teaching them the responsibilities of democratic citizenship, including an understanding of high art. Public television thereby functioned as a cultural technology "meant to help combat what bureaucrats called 'the poverty of the intellect.'"[18] Along these lines, the Corporation for Public Broadcasting's American History and Civics Initiative promoted *Mission US* as one of its key offerings to educational institutions, noting that the video game form can reach students where other formats have failed: "*Mission US* adapts the most popular emerging technology in young people's lives—gaming—to immerse them in the drama of our nation's past."[19] As stated on the *Mission US* website, "*Mission*

US aims to get students to care about history by seeing it through the eyes of peers from the past."[20] The video game form is central to this process, with its promise of fun, interactivity, and immersion.[21]

Racial Immersion

Although it is important to attend to the content and representational politics of games, theorizing gaming requires more than that. It also requires thinking about what it is like to play the game and the way the players make choices and create new narratives as they play. Players navigate choices based on code and algorithms, thereby creating their individual gaming experience. As "procedural representations," games "rely on user interaction as a mediator, something static and moving images cannot claim to do."[22] Games demand active participation, creating meaning through action, in addition to visual and textual meaning.[23] This has implications with respect to race and play. The processual nature of code-based media, including video games, means that players are implicated in the doing in addition to the viewing. Such media executes race, with users performing the images of race that they consume. Performance via play rather than mere consumption connotes a more active engagement with race and media, with the users ostensibly doing race rather than simply consuming it. A player acts out and produces race in the act of playing and interacting with algorithms that also create race. Peter Chow-White terms this the "informationalization of race," where information that emerges "through the digital space of communication networks, computer codes, computational algorithms, and databases" constitutes a "new regime of racial signification."[24] This new racial formation relies on the "seeming neutrality of digital space" to reduce bodies and practices to code, reinscribing biological notions of race.[25] As such, Lisa Nakamura and Chow-White argue that scholars "must attend to how race operates as a set of parameters and affordances, ideological activities, and programmed codes."[26] Race is embedded in games in multiple ways: at the levels of programming, code, and representation, as well as within user interaction and play. This is intensified in the context of an educational game, particularly one about the history of U.S. chattel slavery. What subjects is such a game meant to produce? What is at stake when race, however unacknowledged, is played as a means toward identification?

It is certainly not a new idea that racial understanding is best inculcated through embodiment. Such attempts to apprehend racial oppression most often feature white people endeavoring to embody Blackness, including 1961's *Black Like Me* and the 2006 reality TV program *Black. White.*, where a Black family and a white family "become" white and Black, respectively, through makeup and wigs. In Indiana, the Follow the North Star program at Conner Prairie Living History Museum promises its participants immersion and "intense, living drama" as they play runaway slaves "working together to navigate the Underground Railroad to freedom."[27] These social experiments are premised on a host of assumptions about race, affect, knowledge, and truth, with supposed embodiment guaranteeing the most authentic access to experiencing white supremacist oppression in order to (presumably) instill empathy.[28] *Flight to Freedom* likewise promulgates these narratives about racial embodiment and the fostering of empathy. The promotional materials emphasize that the game is able to make slavery "come alive" in ways previously unavailable by even visual forms like documentary or television. This, in turn, is tied to achieving better learning outcomes. According to one of the game's press releases, "Research has shown that, by assuming the roles of peers from the past, students develop a more personal, memorable, and meaningful connection with complex historical content and context."[29] Playing a role-playing edugame is justified by the personal connection it yields, which is presumed to be significant for learning about "complex" history. Role-playing or inhabiting someone else—a "peer"—supposedly results in better comprehension.

Flight to Freedom purports to immerse players not just in the video game diegesis but also in the life of an enslaved person; players inhabit Lucy and, according to the game's promotional materials, "become a slave." In the game's introductory video geared toward educators, *Mission US* adviser Christopher Moore states, "The game makes possible an answer to a very difficult question: what was it like to be a slave? And the game is about the choices that people made to bring about their own emancipation." Later in the video, he continues, "As a descendant of slaves, I felt very moved by this game. It allowed us to meet, to help, to become a slave. That helps us understand history a whole lot better."[30] Moore's mention of his ancestry, which certainly informs his experience of the game, also works to lend authenticity to the game and simultaneously provides a shield from criticism that *Flight to Freedom* is offensive to Black Americans in particular. His claim that the immersive nature of the game yields a better understanding of history reveals the significance of the role-playing format and positions edugames—specifically the putative embodiment and interactivity they offer—as an answer to "understanding" slavery.[31] This has the secondary effect of yielding better appreciation of how "Americans struggled to realize the ideals of liberty and equality," a stated learning goal of *Mission US*.[32] The linkage of immersion and historical understanding is an aim of living history museums, but the larger discourse about producing good citizens via gaming is indebted to the notion that games yield a form of empathy only possible through embodiment and the "doing" of race as one plays.

For example, in the introductory video to *Flight to Freedom*, teacher Diane Murray underscores what she sees as the connection between embodiment, immersion, and understanding. After shots of her sixth-grade students playing *Flight to Freedom* in the classroom, Murray explains, "I've always taught the subject of slavery, but this game really made it come alive. A lot of times they might read a passage about slavery and think, 'How could you let someone treat you that way? I would never do that.' And then, with this game, they really see how difficult an enslaved person's life really was."[33] Through the role-playing, interactive form, *Flight to Freedom* putatively provides students with empathetic understanding and offers an implicit rejoinder to the notion that enslaved people were complacent. As such, the game operates as a "mode of redress," where "the claims of the past upon the present are registered in terms of stolen 'agency' and addressed through the writing of history which returns that 'agency' to its rightful owners. Or, more accurately, through accounts which represent that agency being as returned, since the rightful owners in question have long since passed on."[34] *Flight to Freedom*'s focus on "returning" agency to enslaved Black people thus has a twofold impetus: as a remedy, it forecloses other possibilities. By restoring agency, the game offers its student players a sense of completion with respect to slavery and its legacies in the United States. If students have internalized the game's lesson, including increased "respect for African Americans' struggle," the "mission" has been completed; there is no need for reparations of any sort. Simply through better appreciating enslaved agency, the ideal neoliberal multicultural citizen-subject does not need to think about slavery further.

Moreover, one of the central claims for *Mission US* in particular and edugames more broadly is that they offer a solution to reach "struggling learners who have difficulty learning from a textbook."[35] According to a *Flight to Freedom* teacher's guide, serious games are uniquely positioned as an "effective way to teach about sensitive topics such as human rights, the war on terror, immigration, and environmental crises," although no specifics are offered about why exactly serious games are especially suited for "sensitive topics" other than the implicit presumption that making learning "fun" will alleviate possible tensions arising from complex and potentially controversial topics.[36] The gamification of the history of slavery has been a key point of criticism for *Flight to Freedom*, yet it is not the first edugame about slavery. In 1995, the parents of an eleven-year-old Black student sued an Arizona school district over the classroom use of the computer game *Freedom!* where players start as enslaved southerners trying to acquire literacy skills in order to escape to the north. Players first inhabit the role of an unlettered enslaved man referred to by the enslaver as "boy." According to the lawsuit, the character Grandfather Cato "has lines written on the computer screen like this: 'I sees a runnin' look in yo' eyes, chile. How c'n I help?'" A parents' group in Indiana objected to the game's representation of Black people, as well as to its presentation to students—the game was offered as something "students could explore in their free time" without accompanying curriculum.[37] The game, withdrawn from the market in 1993 with the software company stating that "it had instructed school districts to destroy any copies they had," was deleted from Arizona school district computers.[38] Other contemporary edugames about slavery include National Geographic's *The Underground Railroad* and the extremely controversial (and horrific) *Playing History 2: Slave Trade*, a game developed by Denmark's Serious Games Interactive that included a "Slave Tetris" segment where players stacked and arranged enslaved people into the hold of a slave ship.[39]

Public outrage expressed on platforms such as Twitter resulted in the game's developers removing that portion of the game. *Flight to Freedom* differs from *Freedom!* not just in terms of design sophistication but also because of its relationship to public media, which constitutes *Flight to Freedom* as a game that rigorously engages historical scholarship; as such, it is constructed as serious and authoritative, and therefore more educationally valuable and historically accurate.

Building Empathetic Citizens through Edugaming

Flight to Freedom's focus on instilling empathy in students is part of a larger movement to develop games for "good," an implicit rejoinder to broader cultural anxieties about digital media, and games in particular, as sapping the ability to empathize with others. Combined with a focus on race, this affective governance draws on a much longer history (as demonstrated in the previous chapters) of the idea that addressing racism stems primarily from a lack of empathy. Interest in games as a cultural technology capable of shaping and modifying behavior has given rise to social science research on their efficacy.[40]

Edugames are part of a burgeoning cadre of what Ian Bogost terms "serious games," although the terminology varies within industry, academic, and popular literature.[41] Such games are created to promote institutional agendas—including in the realms of education, government, and the military—and although Bogost sees possibility for gamers to play against the ideological grain of a game's creators, he suggests that serious games are often produced in order to perpetuate the status quo of "political, corporate, and social institutions."[42] For instance, *America's Army*, a first-person shooter (FPS) developed, funded, and maintained by the U.S. Army, is used as a marketing tool to recruit and train soldiers for the U.S. military. Free to download, *America's Army* relies on the FPS genre to combine public relations and "propaganda elements" with play so as to recruit under the auspices of a depoliticized game.[43] Although *Mission US* differs greatly from *America's Army* in its presentation and aims, it similarly functions to further the particular educational goals and interests of WNET and its collaborating partners.[44]

There has been a larger impetus to use games as tools of affective governance to "improve children's sociability, schoolwork and overall behavior," particularly increasing empathy for others—this is the broader context in which I situate *Flight to Freedom*.[45] This "gaming for good" attempts to "mold the psyche": game development is informed by social scientists, including psychologists like Melissa DeRosier, the CEO of the 3C Institute (formerly the 3-C Institute for Social Development), a company that "creates evidence-based programs and web-based applications to promote health and well-being," namely in schools and clinics.[46] The nonprofit Games for Change, founded in 2004, has been central to the funding and development of what the organization calls "social impact" games, and it cosponsored the 2015 Games for Learning summit with the U.S. Department of Education.[47]

In a *Newsweek* article about what author Elizabeth Svoboda describes as "socially conscious games," Iowa State University psychologist Douglas Gentile underscores the behaviorist angle of serious games: "'Games are Skinner boxes: You do a behavior, you either get rewarded or you get punished. We're training ways of perceiving and thinking about the world.'"[48] This is abundantly clear in *Flight to Freedom*, where a "wrong" choice or behavior results in Lucy remaining enslaved or sent further south. Serious games act as a technology of neoliberal governance, molding the conduct and emotions of players within the game in order to shape it in the "real" world. For example, the U.S. Department of Education has funded games like *Zoo U* to "teach social skills on a national scale," which include behaving in accordance with mainstream norms of decorum: "When 3C researchers did a trial of *Zoo U* with a group of 7- to 11-year-olds, kids who'd played the game felt more socially confident afterward, behaved less aggressively and were better able to regulate their emotions."[49] According to the 3C Institute's website, *Zoo U* requires players to "navigate social situations with other characters in an engaging virtual school for zookeepers in training. *Zoo U* focuses on six core social skills: impulse control, empathy, initiation, communication, cooperation, and emotion regulation."[50] In an article on the effectiveness of *Zoo U*, DeRosier et al. argue that a lack of "social skills competence can increase children's risk for poor adjustment across many areas of functioning," including "delinquency and antisocial behavior" and "substance abuse."[51] *Zoo U* and other edugames attempt to intervene in and mediate risk through affective governance.[52]

Mission US adds an overt civic dimension to this discourse on the social benefits of edugames. In a PBS NewsHour article promoting *Mission US*, the author cites a study on the benefits of games published in the American Psychological Association's journal, *American Psychologist.* The study claims that the "right" games can foster "a sense of community and positive predispositions toward civic engagement." To support this claim, the study references earlier research "showing those who participate in massively multiplayer online role-playing games (MMPORGs) are more likely to be engaged in social and civic movements in their everyday lives, such as raising more for charity, volunteering, voting and persuading others to do the same."[53] In other words, the right games, a category in which PBS firmly situates *Mission US*, help to shape exemplary citizens who participate in their communities in ways unthreatening to the status quo, who stay in school, and who feel the appropriate feelings.

Moreover, the ideal neoliberal citizen-subject is characterized in part by an ability to successfully navigate an array of choices.[54] Choice is the animating structure of *Flight to Freedom*, including in the realm of emotion: Lucy must choose how to manage her feelings of anger and hopelessness as described during the game's prologue. Here, the player is introduced to Lucy, who describes her daily labor: "I get up before the sun and I'm still working after it goes down. It's worst at harvest time. Almost all the other folks are out in the fields. So, I gotta collect the eggs, and do the wash, fetch water, feed the hogs, scrub the pots, and even more than that." Next, the player meets Mr. Otis, the white overseer; Lucy explains that he "works us hard." Everyone is a faceless outline reminiscent of the work of artist Kara Walker, who uses the nineteenth-century form of cut-paper silhouettes in her tableaux about slavery. After Lucy tells the player, "Some folks try to get by, to not get beat, to keep their families together," her shadowy outline is filled in with facial features and she is visibly angry:

> But lots of times, I get mad. Other folks do too. They get back at Master King in different ways. Some do their work slow. Some break things. Some run away for a while, like Henry. I turned 14 last month and Mama said, now that I'm grown up,

things will be harder on me. How can they get any harder?
I wish things were different, but what can I do? What can a
slave do?

From here, the game cuts to a screen with a list of options under
"What can I do? What can a slave do?":

> Lucy's Journey Badges
> Play it safe?
> Commit an act of resistance?
> Or sabotage the King Plantation?
> These are some of the decisions you will face as you
> guide Lucy through the game. Remember there is no "right"
> answer, but some of the choices you make will have lasting
> consequences. As you make choices, you unlock Journey
> Badges that you will use to determine Lucy's ultimate jour-
> ney in the game's epilogue. At the end of each part you will
> see which badges you unlocked . . . and which you did not.

As such, Lucy's freedom depends on the badges one collects throughout the game. Players earn badges by navigating four options for
Lucy's response to particular situations and by viewing highlighted
"smartwords," which take the player to a definition. During one game,
I selected the "resistance" option for each situation, choosing, for
example, to have Lucy steal some eggs, which resulted in the following screen: "You got the Resistance Badge. You acted against Master
King. By working slowly, disobeying orders or destroying his property you are fighting, or resisting, slavery. Will he find out? Will you
get punished? Will you resist more?" When I had Lucy continue
to resist, she was eventually sent down south and the game ended
before I completed the second section. In order to advance in the
game, one must combine the resistance badge with other badges and
skills, including "persuasion," "playing it safe," and "literacy." During
one game, I earned a "self-reliant" badge for running away by myself,
with the screen reading, "You set out by yourself, determined to find
freedom," thus rewarding me for taking personal responsibility over
Lucy's welfare.

Flight to Freedom's lessons include an explicit focus on teaching cause and effect and encouraging "perspective-taking, discussion, and weighing of multiple kinds of evidence."[55] Players must consider the possible consequences of Lucy's actions as a runaway. For example, when I chose to have Lucy float across the river on a log, a screen warned me that it was "very risky": "You drag a log into the water and start paddling. It is very difficult and tiring to fight the river current. About halfway across you give up paddling. It's all you can do to hold on. The river sweeps you away." Lucy's only option is "pray." After clicking on "pray," the screen reads, "Amazingly, you don't drown. You are plucked out of the water by the crew of a flatboat. They tie you up and turn you over to the sheriff in Dover." Upon capture, the game ends and I am offered another chance to try part two. Students are taught to properly manage risk in a world where choices are simplified and certain options are not even offered. When they fail, players must start over and try again.

Black Agency and White Complicity

By relying on a neoliberal notion of agency (that goes unmarked as such) and tethering "humanity" to "agency" to "resistance," *Flight to Freedom* expunges the "forms of human 'agency' which can in no way be seen as resistant to slavery, specifically collaboration and betrayal."[56] I want to be very clear that my critique of *Flight to Freedom*'s emphasis on agency centers primarily on the reproduction of (neo) liberal selfhood and the attendant erasure of white supremacy and racial capitalism's role in chattel slavery.[57] It is worth reiterating that this occurs within a state-funded video game geared toward shaping youth—some of whom are considered "risky"—into ideal U.S. citizen-subjects in part through affective governance. Forms of liberalism, including neoliberalism, have always been grounded in whiteness; *Flight to Freedom* alters the foundation of liberalism (white freedom produced through Black unfreedom) by attempting to restore agency to Blackness via the eradication of both fear and white terror toward Black people. As a result, whiteness is liberal (agential, free), but such agency is not constituted in relation to Black subjection given that the role of white supremacy in the latter is simply expunged. This neoliberal maneuver is one of incorporation through erasure: the game seeks to fold Blackness into liberal agency, but to do so obscures how this category is dependent on white complicity in chattel slavery.

In *Flight to Freedom*, the focus on recuperating African American agency is accompanied by a complete erasure of white collusion in slavery, which is a form of agency that falls outside the bounds of agency as necessarily resistive. White people's daily decisions, actions, and thoughts produced, reproduced, and supported slavery. Angela Davis notes that enslavers, who "maintained an absolute monopoly of violence," were able to count on "large numbers of their fellow white men . . . to assist them in their terrorist machinations," without whom slavery would have "been far less feasible."[58] Agency, thus, is not only resistance to power. To use an uncritical agency framework to teach about the history of U.S. chattel slavery while simultaneously leaving unacknowledged white culpability or white supremacy in any sense reproduces a neoliberal subjectivity that both relies on and disavows whiteness. An uncomplicated and celebratory definition of *agency* fails to consider the category's entanglement with liberalism and the liberal subject, both of which are inseparable from whiteness. Liberal subjectivity, Amber Jamilla Musser explains, is "founded on the premise of ascendancy into whiteness."[59] The type of liberal subjectivity I reference in this chapter differs from the liberal subjectivity of the 1960s, which valorized a white, male, middle-class ideal. Here, I envision subjectivity as bound up with multiculturalism and postrace discourse and informed by neoliberalism. Ideal neoliberal subjects are self-enterprising and beyond race.

Centralizing the "experience—and agency—of African Americans" and bringing "to life the everyday forms of resistance undertaken by enslaved communities" is one of *Flight to Freedom*'s primary aims.[60] As noted in a press release defending the game, *Flight to Freedom* "tells some ugly truths about slavery" but it also "aims to humanize enslaved people and present them with dignity, courage, fear, and real human emotions like love and hate." The release continues:

> The mission portrays enslaved African Americans with
> agency and personal power (even when social, economic,
> and political power was non-existent), and as central actors

in their own destinies. Our goal is for all students to develop
a greater respect for African Americans' struggle and African
American history as a part of American history.[61]

Given that *Mission US* was informed by social history scholarship
seeking to feature the experiences of those typically ignored by historical scholarship, it is unsurprising that *Flight to Freedom* takes on
this emphasis in an attempt to center new perspectives. Yet, in the
context of an educational video game produced partly as a means to
help solve the crisis of U.S. high school dropouts (a racialized and
classed phenomenon) by making learning fun, it is significant that
the game, which also strives to teach certain civic values, centers
agency, a key category for neoliberal subjectivity and whiteness.[62] As
noted in the teacher's guide:

> Lucy must make important decisions along the way. Should
> she travel in more settled areas, with better roads but more
> people, or in wooded areas that are difficult to navigate but
> have less chance of being spotted? What should she say if she
> encounters a slave catcher? What will she wish she had taken
> from the plantation? Each of these decisions will impact
> whether Lucy successfully makes her way north or is cap-
> tured and re-enslaved.[63]

Agency is individualized and strategic in a personal sense—it is not
collaborative resistance. Lucy might wish for something different to
help her escape, implying a possible poor choice on her part. Teachers are thus guided to emphasize choice and only Lucy's choices in
particular, never the choices of white characters to capture, enslave,
rape, police, and terrorize.

   Walter Johnson's essay "On Agency" is instructive here. Johnson
details how new social historians working on slavery understand
their research and scholarship as a way to "'give the slaves back their
agency,'" thereby becoming "the master trope around which historians understand arguments about slavery."[64] The primary contribution is to "recover agency," something that Johnson argues should
actually be the basic foundation for historical inquiry rather than the
end goal of the scholarship.[65] Framing the work as a "discovery" of

Black humanity and agency (which get conflated) reproduces the very thing that historians ostensibly want to repudiate: the notion that enslaved people were docile. Further, Johnson details how the collapse of humanity into agency "formulates enslaved people's actions in much too abstract a manner," ignoring the specificity of the social, political, and cultural context of the time.[66] Yet, this erasure of particularity is evident in the very categories themselves, not just their application. Johnson writes, "The term 'agency' smuggles a notion of the universality of a liberal notion of selfhood, with its emphasis on independence and choice, right into the middle of a conversation about slavery against which that supposed natural (at least for white men) condition was originally defined."[67] Simply put, liberal subjectivity required Black unfreedom to demarcate the category of liberalism and its attendant racial formation, whiteness. According to Johnson, historians often fail to consider what humanity might mean outside "the conventions of liberal agency." What, in other words, would a "slave humanity" look like?[68]

Considering the broader context impinging upon racial formation, especially the rise of digital media, illuminates how the discourse of interactivity is brought to bear on our understandings of race, emotion, and white supremacy. Although Johnson is critical of how many historians of slavery use agency as a framework for their scholarship, he notes that this emphasis arose out of the activist context of the 1960s and 1970s and as such, framing "Black humanity as self-determination and resistance" was powerful in that particular era.[69] The civil rights era marked a significantly different institutional environment from the one in which he wrote the essay in 2003; in the latter, institutions celebrate multicultural inclusion while racialized and gendered forms of exploitation proliferate globally. Johnson thus urges historians of slavery to ask different questions of the archive— ones that widen an occluded field of vision—rather than returning to agency as the paradigmatic framework of historical scholarship on slavery. Similarly, in her discussion of what the archive produces and erases, historian Stephanie Smallwood underscores the politics of knowledge that undergird the "writing of histories of modern racial slavery"—not the archive alone "but rather the critical philosophical assumptions that shape and structure our understandings of history."[70] In terms of race and racial formation, *Flight to Freedom*'s emergence in 2011 differs markedly from 2003 in a multitude of ways, including the rapid proliferation of digital technologies. Contrary to mainstream imaginings of code and algorithms—the backbones of digital culture—as race neutral or postrace, scholars have demonstrated how race absolutely informs new technologies and platforms and, indeed, is inextricable from them.[71] The emphasis on race neutrality reinforces a colorblind technological fetishism that erases the devastating material effects of racialized algorithms.[72]

Such technological fetishism—the idea that technology is the solution to complex issues, including racism and white supremacy—cannot be disentangled from the algorithmic rationalities and temporalities of *Flight to Freedom*. The game's multiple temporalities, including the postbellum era in the epilogue, reproduce a progress narrative without mentioning the ongoing logics and effects of chattel slavery in the contemporary era. The mission ends, and once completed, agency is ostensibly bestowed across a population. Given that, as Walter Johnson emphasizes, the restoration of agency occurs to people no longer living, whom does this serve? And toward what end, other than the reproduction of liberal subjectivity as agential?

A Painless Landscape

Although *Flight to Freedom*'s emphasis is on inculcating empathy, some player reviews mentioned fear as the primary affective experience during game play. One, in particular, connected this to immersion, noting that the game is both engaging and a "harrowing, illuminating look at the realities of life as an American slave. I was struck by how effectively the game placed me in the shoes of an American slave. The precarious nature of my existence was readily apparent. The game's presentational simplicity forced me to use my imagination, and I imagined very scary things."[73] Although the reviewer is correct that the aesthetics of the game are quite simple, it is interesting that he connects the sparse visuals to stimulating his imagination and creating a fear-invoking diegesis, thereby fleshing out the game's narrative. I had the opposite experience when I played the game, which I did multiple times. *Flight to Freedom* creates an antebellum world where it is not rape and sexual violence, torture, and white terrorism that constitute Black bondage but rather an occasional whipping, which is referenced but never shown. The reviewer notes that he kept reminding himself, "This was real. . . . People lived this, they lived under these laws and with this kind of fear. Sneaking through the yard at night, stealing enough food from the garden to be able to survive the coming trial . . . I was very much in the moment. It was intense."[74] This reviewer repeatedly emphasizes the affective dimensions of game play—it was harrowing, scary, intense—yet I found *Flight to Freedom* actually devoid of much affective intensity at all, and certainly nowhere near the affective flow that characterizes *Roots* and its anticipated catharsis. Scholars like Aubrey Anable and Alexander Galloway have underscored the centrality of affect to gaming, with Anable noting that although video games "compel us to act (and to be acted upon) through the procedures of their algorithmic structure," the action is made visible through images that also inform our actions via their affective pull: "In a very basic sense, we make choices and push buttons in games because of how games structure our feelings about those choices and actions."[75] Yet *Flight to Freedom* felt clinical and distant. During game play, there is no music, nor any sound other than a slot machine–like chime to indicate when Lucy has earned a badge or eaten food and the clicking of the mouse to make choices. *Flight to Freedom* is, after all, a game, and so much of what drives the player is not fear but rather a desire to succeed and move to the next level. One of the review questions in the teacher's guide—"What is the King plantation like? What are some things you saw and heard?"—presumes a diegesis that is much more richly fleshed out.

Despite its claims to embodiment, *Flight to Freedom*'s presentational aspects are such that the player is rarely given a first-person view of events. Rather, the player most frequently views Lucy from a bird's-eye view and thus a place of omniscience as one moves a button-like circular avatar of her around on a map. In this way, the player is actually quite distanced from the events of the game, which appear instead as reductive, sanitized, and painless. For instance, one of Lucy's initial community tasks (which are distinct from the plantation tasks that are given by white people) is to get comfrey root by the creek for her mother, who is tending to Henry, an enslaved man who was whipped the previous evening. When the enslaver

Mr. Otis catches Lucy, she is given three plantation tasks and a stern rebuke. Yet the player can simply choose to try going to the creek again. When Lucy finishes a task, a badge lights up on the screen, accompanied by a sound indicating completion, offering the player the sense of crossing something off a to-do list and the attendant small pleasure of doing so.

The avatar glides seamlessly across the map, an empty landscape devoid of people and much of anything, save the occasional farm. I played the game multiple times and only occasionally did Lucy encounter a slave patrol, from which I could have her hide. Further, within the game, the choices are quite circumscribed, with Lucy's options highlighted on the map.

Even moments that are included presumably for their affective pull are dulled by the game's aesthetic, sonic, and representational choices. When I have Lucy go to the Preston plantation to see her father and seek his assistance, the screen reads, "Your father is overjoyed to see you. When you explain your situation, his manner turns grim. He gives you some food and tells you to find his brother up north at the Skinner farm. He hugs you goodbye and wipes away a tear." The only option offered Lucy is to "say goodbye and leave." There is neither music nor images of their interaction to accompany Lucy's father's statement. The game relies instead on exposition to mitigate its dull and emotionless landscape. When I hear dogs at one point, I decide to keep walking rather than "run for it!" The following screen pops up: "You keep walking. The sound fades away, but you still feel very nervous." The sole option is to "move on." Later, when crossing a river, I am told, "You make it to the far side of the ford without any trouble. That was nerve-wracking!" Because there is nothing to show, the player must be told what to feel in a sanitized, reductive, and painless diegesis.

Sanitized Whiteness

Flight to Freedom's substitution of fear and terror with nerves and anxiety underscores the absolute minimization of white violence in the game. White people, and white men especially, were empowered to surveil, threaten, police, and capture anyone they considered an enslaved person on the run (to say nothing of the quotidian violence endured by enslaved people). This power intensified with the passage of the Fugitive Slave Act in 1850, which *Flight to Freedom* acknowledges in the game's narrative summary. The lack of white men who are anything more than somewhat menacing (if that) reinforces a narrative of white benevolence and the agency underpinning the liberal subject as resistive. Through the game and its accompanying curricula, African Americans are incorporated into (neo)liberal subjectivity via an emphasis on agency and resistance; at the same time, white liberal agency as bound up with the oppression and enslavement of Black people is obfuscated. Simply put, Black agency here occurs in the absence of white (racist) agency. There is no discussion of race or racism in the game or the accompanying curriculum, nor is there any attention to gender, much less Lucy's status as a young Black woman. Sexual violence, in particular, is never mentioned. The teacher's guide's "Top Five Things to Know before You Play" states that these "important pieces of information to consider . . . may or may not help you as Lucy makes her way through life on a plantation in the 1840s," including the following description of the violence central to slavery:

> Slavery was a system based on cruelty and violence. Slaves found ways to resist their masters by working slowly, breaking tools, "stealing" food or clothes, or lying to their masters. All these forms of resistance carried the risk of punishment, which often included whippings. Slaves who tried to run away or were openly rebellious risked severe whippings, branding, imprisonment, or were forced to wear iron collars around their neck, hands, or feet. Slaves that burned property, stole, or committed murder or other serious crimes were killed.[76]

As written, there are no white subjects branding, whipping, imprisoning, torturing, or killing the enslaved. Slaves "were killed" and "risked" punishment.

Further, most of the game's white characters are noble and helpful. For example, Sheriff McKee is described in the character overview as "Ripley's sheriff, who is responsible for maintaining law and order. He is not an abolitionist, but sympathizes with fugitives who are trying to escape. He does not enjoy returning them to slavery." Through recourse to Sheriff McKee's caring and lack of enjoyment, the game positions him as sympathetic even though he is "not an abolitionist." Rather, he is just doing his job and adhering to his responsibilities— maintaining law and order. Such a description renders him passive, compliant, and as merely caught up in a system; he is not framed as an actor with agency who is making choices but instead as someone who has liberal guilt. Such guilt operates as what Musser calls a "racialized performance of passivity" that produces a complex innocence "constructed through a focus on the suffering that guilt produces, which, in turn, manifests itself as empathy and analogizes the white body's current guilt to the black body's past (and present) trauma. Through empathy, the substitution of the white body for the black body, current guilt or suffering distracts from the choice of inaction and produces color blindness."[77] This description of Sheriff Ripley as someone who "does not enjoy" returning Black people to slavery (yet who does it anyway) implicitly invokes sympathy for him based on his own suffering, understood as his lack of enjoyment.

Many of the other white characters in *Flight to Freedom* are portrayed as harmless. When Lucy passes a white man on the road (and I chose to keep going), the screen reads, "The man watches you go. After a moment, he calls after you. 'If you cross the Licking River at the toll bridge, tell Jeb that his brother Heath says "hello.""" The only option offered Lucy is to "thank him and move on." The man does not threaten Lucy but simply wants her to convey greetings to his brother. Later in the game, Lucy meets a white woman, Millie, who appreciates Lucy's directness regarding rescuing her family: "You get right to the point. I like that. Where is your family?" After I chose to ask her to help my family, a message at the bottom of the screen reads, "Millie's opinion of you improves." By including Millie's approval of Lucy's forthrightness, *Flight to Freedom* balances the overtly racist (though never named as such) white people, such as the daughter of Lucy's enslaver, with well-meaning, kindly, and helpful ones who advance the cause of abolition in a plethora of ways. When Lucy asks Millie about buying her family's freedom, Millie responds, "Even if I had that much money, buying their freedom would be supporting the system of slavery. We mustn't give money to our enemies." Millie's patronizing response highlights her moral purity and erases the imbrication of slavery with all aspects of everyday life. For *Flight to Freedom*, a focus on Black agency means an erasure of white complicity and white (racist) agency.

According to WNET and *Flight to Freedom*, one must learn about U.S. history in order to fulfill one's civic duties and to be appropriately versed in the language of liberal agency. Completing the mission means one has successfully internalized the game's lessons, which are framed through nationalist discourses. As one reviewer notes, "Mission U.S. would certainly make for an engaging classroom aid, but it's so much more than that—it's an entertaining, well-made adventure game, a slice of livable history that every American should play."[78] Indeed, the overall learning goals for *Mission US* include learning "the story of America and the ways Americans struggled to realize the ideals of liberty and equality."[79] This story of the United States is one where white supremacy is obscured by the language of liberal agency, heightened by a focus on empathy to the exclusion of other feelings. Through immersion and interactivity, *Flight to Freedom* is part of a longer history of the constitution of white subjectivity through popular pedagogical treatments of the history of U.S. chattel slavery. In *Flight to Freedom*, this occurs through the emphasis on Black agency while simultaneously erasing white agency with respect to slavery and white supremacy. At the same time, the game and accompanying curriculum's emphasis on inculcating admiration, appreciation, and sympathy for "African American struggle" reproduces an asymmetrical power dynamic. According to Musser, "Sympathy demonstrated the humanity of blacks while simultaneously othering them. Perversely, those in possession of sympathy were seen as virtuous, thus further distancing themselves from the objects of their pity."[80] In an era of virtue signaling on social media, where wokeness is cool and becomes a way to self-stylize and self-brand, Musser's point that those "in possession of sympathy" are rewarded for it is brought into sharp focus.

This underscores the entanglement of residual and emergent racial formations in the twenty-first century, where digital and algorithmic culture and their associations with race neutrality intertwine with a performative antiracism often visible on social media. We can thus see the ongoing tension between data and emotion—frequently positioned in opposition—as means to address racialized disparities. *Mission US* is continuing to use digital media to support its efforts; despite the vocal criticism of *Flight to Freedom*, including the critique that the game makes slavery "fun," *Mission US* has developed an app called *Think Fast about the Past!*[81] At present, there are two missions, with the second one requiring players to rescue Lucy's brother Jonah from a plantation by answering questions quickly within a five-minute time frame.

By teaching students a whitewashed version of the history of U.S. chattel slavery, *Flight to Freedom* modifies the aims of *Roots* for the contemporary era, relying on neoliberal discourses of choice and agency, as well as a theorization of race made possible through code. The next chapter will demonstrate the increasing uptake of understandings of race as information, made intelligible through algorithms and data.

CHAPTER 4

"How Many Slaves Work for You?"

Algorithmic Governance and Guilt

During the past decade, the rise of big data, artificial intelligence (AI), and algorithms more generally have intensified the propensity to turn toward data-driven solutions as an appealing color-blind answer to questions of race and racism. Purportedly neutral data, constituted as emotionless and objective, provides the cornerstone of algorithmic governance, the "capture, co-ordination and capitalization of data" in order to manage and govern populations by automated systems that "[regulate] the flows of [our] data and information."[1] Beyond the regulation of data flows, however, algorithmic governance operates as a way to manage difference and establishes new modes of racialized control. This is especially evident in the use of predictive analytics for policing but likewise in the uptake of algorithms to determine everything from insurance rates to housing loans to bail.[2] For instance, activist calls to eliminate cash bail, a system that punishes the poor, have been mollified by algorithmic determination of bail instead, yet this "race-neutral" risk assessment has been found to reproduce racial bias.[3] Contemporary "digital redlining," where insurance companies and banks use algorithms to determine which neighborhoods to invest in and which to avoid, puts a twenty-first-century spin on the types of racial policing of neighborhoods and geographic space visible in chapter 1's documentaries.[4] Given the social construction of technology, it is, of course, unsurprising that algorithms reify existing racialized structures, yet the discourse of race neutrality permeates the uptake of these digital tools, obfuscating their reproduction of racism for a new era.

Although this dichotomy between rationality (as evidenced by data) and emotion has been an ongoing struggle over approaches to race, it has magnified as data and digital tools putatively offer a detached and tidy answer to the supposed messiness and irrationality of emotion. Racism, in other words, is constituted in the technological sublime as an issue of personal bias and human error, one that can be rectified or at least ameliorated through digital technology.[5] Algorithmic governance meets affective governance in the former's emphasis on neutrality and a binarized rendering of data as distinct from emotion. Data is on offer as a means of transcending emotion, which gets articulated to race as another irrational category in need of datafication. Along these lines, the website (and accompanying app) Slavery Footprint—a collaboration between the nonprofit Made in a Free World (formerly Call + Response) and the U.S. State Department—is part of this ushering in of algorithmic solutions to enormous and complex social and economic problems.[6]

Critically, the website and app are explicitly not about emotional catharsis but rather seek to engage users through neoliberal discourse about empowerment and consumption as means to solve "twenty-first century slavery." In this way, the site and app direct and channel emotional responses toward algorithmic answers, reassuring users that technology—and consumer culture—will take care of it. Affective experiences (particularly guilt) are translated into ostensibly neutral data, which in turn is channeled toward so-called ethical consumption as an effective remedy. As the site proclaims, "Want to fight slavery? There's an app for that."[7]

Since the website's release in September 2011, more than twenty-two million people have assessed their "slavery footprint" through the site's survey, which measures consumer reliance on forced labor in the Global South by analyzing one's consumption habits of popular goods like iPhones, clothing, coffee, and so on. In this chapter, I examine Slavery Footprint as part of the broader shift toward algorithmic management of emotion in relation to race. Much like *Flight to Freedom*, interactivity offers a means toward racial "understanding," although Slavery Footprint bypasses any acknowledgment of race altogether in lieu of a transnational and colorblind notion of difference, one where U.S. consumers function as saviors of a racialized other. This is underscored in the site's pedagogical use of the history of U.S. chattel slavery, which is deployed to add moral heft and urgency to address what it calls modern-day or twenty-first-century slavery. In so doing, Slavery Footprint and Made in a Free World lo-

cate slavery elsewhere both temporally and spatially, erasing the afterlife of slavery and the salience of anti-Black racism to everyday life.
Through their reliance on algorithms and data to uncover what
they term "slavery," Made in a Free World and Slavery Footprint
promulgate the notion of the digital as not only neutral and separate
from race and capitalism but also as capable of undoing slavery. By
understanding slavery as embedded in capitalism, I suggest that we
can challenge the site's distinction between free labor and what they
call slavery and, in the process, also challenge the notion of so-called
ethical consumption. I want to be clear that I am focusing on neoliberal ethical consumption, and my critique is not that consumer
activism writ large is always in defense of racial capital. Yet for the
most part, ethical consumption uses inequality, poverty, and environmental degradation as an impetus to expand the consumer world
and ultimately bolster capitalism. Moreover, the production of an
"ethical consumer" is inextricable from the production of whiteness
and from the affective pleasures of feeling ethical. Slavery Footprint,
in other words, does not just assuage guilt and other negative affects
but actively fosters positive feelings—which cannot be disentangled
from a white savior complex—through the use of the app and what it
calls ethical shopping. Generating such "affective rewards of superiority" often occurs within what Paula Ioanide identifies as "shaming
economies," including the widespread shaming of welfare recipients
in the United States that in turn yields a sense of superiority.[8] Slavery
Footprint trades on this in their promotional materials, which emphasize the affective reward of saving a marginalized other. As one
Made in a Free World fundraising email concludes, "The end of slavery is starting to feel very possible. Progress feels good, doesn't it?"[9]
   The algorithmic culture that promotes data and technological
fixes as solutions to complex issues renders race into information and
is part of the broader shift toward colorblindness and postrace discourse.[10] Both are in full effect here, made possible through the supposed neutrality of data. Slavery Footprint adopts this logic: rather
than using imagery or photographs to underscore the appalling conditions under which many labor, the site modifies older techniques
from earlier ethical consumption campaigns, drawing instead on a
slickly produced site devoid of images of actual people. Ethical consumption in the United States began during the nineteenth-century

slave trade with the rise of the "free produce" movement, which did not shy away from using images as a persuasive and educational tool.[11] On Slavery Footprint, by contrast, colorblindness is combined with consumption, with Made in a Free World promoting a "more enlightened form of consumerism" as a rejoinder to critiques of white saviorism.[12] As noted on a Made in a Free World–approved business site, "This isn't charity. It's the power of our purchase," a caveat to underscore how this is agency expressed through the market rather than an asymmetrical charitable relation.[13]

Neoliberal Consumer Activism and Racial Formation

During the past decade, a rich body of scholarship on ethical (or radical) consumption and consumer activism has emerged to consider the changing dynamics of consumer citizenship in the neoliberal era.[14] This work has responded to the explosion of a niche of consumer goods, activist and charitable campaigns, and marketing aimed at a so-called ethical consumer concerned with the social, economic, and/or environmental conditions and impact of commodities and their production. Media culture has been central to this process, with a similar rise of television shows (*Blood, Sweat, and T-Shirts; Eco Trip; Consumed*), films (*King Corn; Super Size Me; Fast Food Nation; Food, Inc.*), books (*The Omnivore's Dilemma; Conscious Capitalism*), and lifestyle websites, blogs, and social media influencers seeking to produce, advise, and discipline a conscious, ethical consumer-citizen. The proliferation of brand cultures—including the imperative to effectively self-brand—has likewise made brand relationships a key framework for identity and everyday life.[15] Alongside corporate social responsibility, political brand cultures, which are bound up with consumer activism, encourage "consumers who act politically" within these contexts to "see themselves as activists" in relation to consumption practices.[16] The context of brand cultures is thus one in which, as Sarah Banet-Weiser notes, "'ethical' consumers emerge."[17] This ethical consumer can also be understood as part of a "progressive" or "humanitarian" capitalism that scholars like Paula Chakravartty and Sreela Sarkar identify as an incipient approach to development in the Global South. Drawing our attention to how such formations operate in India, Chakravartty and Sarkar demonstrate that "liberation for the masses through the market" has become the operative mode of poverty management via neoliberal reforms.[18] The emergence of this type of political response to economic injustice can be situated within a cultural and economic context that foregrounds the role of the individual consumer. Slavery Footprint thus operates in tandem with development policies that emphasize "conscious" capitalism, with the Global South's racialized poor providing a new market.[19] Slavery Footprint and Made in a Free World put a new twist on this by constituting global north consumers as "modern-day abolitionists" who purchase freedom for a racialized other. Made in a Free World, the nonprofit responsible for the site, relies on this logic for their fundraising emails, which explain that children in Ghana can be "set on the path to freedom" with "your donation."[20]

Marx's theory of commodity fetishism is instructive here, given its emphasis on making sense of obscured relations of production—this is the putative aim of ethical consumption, which seeks in some instances to defetishize the social nature of the commodity's production. For Slavery Footprint and Made in a Free World, algorithms are the means toward such clarity. Yet as Marx makes clear, demystification is not sufficient—that is, a critique of ideology will not fix this problem of appearance by merely defetishizing the commodity's conditions of production. As such, different strands of ethical consumption offer varying solutions for going beyond demystification, including abstaining from consumption (voluntary simplicity), creating alternatives (No Sweat, American Apparel, Reformation), and putting pressure on corporations to alter their supply chains, as is the case with Slavery Footprint. By making visible the labor conditions behind particular products, brands like American Apparel participate in what Jo Littler and Liz Moor term "fetishized de-fetishization": the production of value (and hence, capital) by foregrounding exploitation and distancing the brand from it.[21] Many types of so-called green consumption and their attendant brands trade on a similar logic. Because it is a collaborative effort between the U.S. State Department and a nonprofit, the website—at least in this incarnation—is not yet directly profiting by making visible exploitation, although it similarly presumes (as does all ethical consumption) that consumers will do something upon learning about conditions of production.

Implicit in this assumption is the idea that consumers will "rescue" racialized and gendered workers in the Global South by consuming more ethically, thus reinforcing the colonial dynamic ethical consumption purportedly attempts to undo. Within this dynamic, the ethical consumer operates through a discourse of whiteness where whiteness is equated with benevolence, care, and ethics. Producing an ethical consumer relies on its unethical counterpart, one who cannot be bothered to care enough to purchase the correct goods, a narrative made explicit in the ethical home products line If You Care.[22] Although ethical consumption has been critiqued for its exclusions—class-based and otherwise—attention to affect highlights what it in fact produces: namely, positive feelings or, at base, the deferral or even erasure of negative ones like guilt. As such, Slavery Footprint is more than an instance of a white savior complex, in part because of the larger context of both neoliberal consumer activism and algorithmic governance. Made in a Free World and Slavery Footprint are aware of a predisposition toward guilt but soothe that by underscoring the power of consumption and algorithms to eradicate modern-day slavery.

Akin to the emphasis on white comfort present in ABC's concerns for white viewers of *Roots,* Slavery Footprint is careful not to render its users too culpable. Although the site implicates consumers to a certain extent and demonstrates a belief in the power of consumers to influence the market, site founder Justin Dillon said: "I didn't want to create another bummer calculator that only spits out bad news. I wanted to see how we can help individuals use their lifestyles to end this."[23] This is repeated throughout the nonprofit's promotional materials, marking an anticipatory caretaking of what Robin DiAngelo terms "white fragility," wherein white people defend against challenges (or even conversations) about race by displaying "emotions such as anger, fear, and guilt."[24] The site echoes Dillon's approach, explaining to survey takers, "That's why we'd like to help you understand your influence on slavery. Not so you can feel bad. Not so you'll stop buying stuff . . . so you will ask the brands you like to find out where their materials are coming from."[25] The attempt to affectively hook users through guilt is tempered by an emphasis on easy solutions and taking care to not overwhelm participants. Through this focus and the colorblind production of difference as geographically distant—over there, not here—Slavery Footprint and Made in a Free World sidestep white fragility because whiteness and white supremacy are not even in question.[26] Such distancing emphasizes feeling empowered rather than complicit, made plain through the presumed freedom to make different consumer choices. Explaining the site, Dillon highlights his belief in consumers as the driving force of the market: "Really the goal is to amplify the conversation between the consumer and the producer. Our torches and pitchforks are out for the slave traders, not the multinationals."[27] One of the solutions is to send a prewritten letter to companies inquiring about the source of their materials; doing so will earn one "Free World points," adding to the gamification aspect of the site not entirely afield from the gamification discussed in chapter 3.

Consuming Freedom

Slavery Footprint works to educate consumers via text interspersed throughout the survey—there are no images of actual people. Instead, the slickly produced site relies on sparse design and strangely lighthearted formulations of disturbing statistics: "There are at least 27 million slaves worldwide. That's roughly the combined population of Australia and New Zealand. Crikey!"
Others include:

Everyone in Orlando walks into a kiln.
In 2007, Save the Children reported that 250,000 children live and work in Pakistani brick kilns in complete social isolation. That's more than the population of Irvine, California, Baton Rouge, Louisiana, or Orlando, Florida.

Shrimp Cocktail, Anyone?
Bonded labor is used for much of Southeast Asia's shrimping industry, which supplies more shrimp to the United States

than to any other country. Laborers work up to 20-hour days to peel 40 pounds of shrimp. Those who attempt to escape are under constant threat of violence or sexual assault.

How do I look in this dirt?
Every day tens of thousands of American women buy makeup. Every day tens of thousands of Indian children mine mica, which is the little sparklies in the makeup.[28]

Although Slavery Footprint is attempting to draw attention to what it terms slavery, these brief descriptions offer the most insight into the supply chain and conditions of production on the site. Most of the site features the survey, to which the homepage directs users by offering two answers in response to the question, "How many slaves work for you?": "What? Slaves work for me?" and "Find out. Take the survey." Once the survey begins, the questions range from asking about how much one uses technology, to the types of food one eats, to the clothing that one buys. Survey takers can earn "Free World points" for each scripted letter they email to a brand of their choice telling them "I want to know" regarding their labor practices.

Like other forms of consumer-based activism, Slavery Footprint considers the individual consumer to be a powerful force in altering the conditions of the market. The proliferation of ethical consumption over the past decade belies a form of activism that has a much longer history within the United States than some scholars of consumption acknowledge. Not just a twentieth-century practice, consumer activism was a tool for antislavery activists during the nineteenth century and included boycotts of slave-made products as well as the creation of "Free Labor" stores. Lawrence Glickman historicizes U.S. consumer activism through his examination of the mid-1800s "free produce" movement, one that he argues "laid the template of modern consumer activism" by its emphasis on the provenance of goods. Similar to Slavery Footprint, this movement emphasized creating an alternative to slave-made products rather than encouraging nonconsumption; activists viewed the market as "an important arena of moral influence subject to their agency" and were the first to suggest "labeling ethical goods." By centering consumption as a prime site of struggle against chattel slavery, the free produce movement figured consumers as "agents of moral and economic change," thereby constituting the "conscientious" (or, in contemporary parlance, "ethical") consumer.[29] Moreover, the free produce movement viewed consumers as the actors who solely dictated the whims of the market, a belief reflected in their key framework: "If there were no consumers of slave-produce, there would be no slaves." This emphasis on consumer sovereignty, Glickman notes, meant that the enslaver and slave trader were expunged from accountability. The guilty, in other words, were not the enslavers but rather the consumers who kept them in business.[30]

In order to create demand for alternatives, free produce activists attempted to defetishize slave-made products by teaching consumers to visualize the horrors of slavery—"the slave's unseen suffering, to see a blood-stained product, and to hear the groans of its maker."[31] Slavery Footprint, by contrast, does not use any visuals of racialized suffering. Rather, the site's attempts at defetishization are limited to the survey's interspersed text, which provides context for the questions the survey asks; there are no photos, videos, or interviews, nor do we hear from anyone from the Global South.[32] Distinct from the affective appeal of *Roots* and visual melodrama, Slavery Footprint's minimal and "cool" aesthetic shares similarities with *Flight to Freedom* in its detached distance. But unlike *Flight to Freedom*, the site does not ask users to imagine themselves as an enslaved person or as a forced laborer. Slavery Footprint and Made in a Free World focus less on empathy and more on producing an individual ethical consumer, aligning with a broader, rational algorithmic culture in which the site is situated.

Defending the Market

Slavery Footprint and Made in a Free World's defense of the market and the "multinationals" marks another key distinction from the free produce movement. The latter did not consider markets themselves as moral but instead viewed them as a prime driver of "moral change." Through the market, "consumers could abet the crime of slavery or eliminate it." Free produce advocates thus presumed that if demand were significant enough, free enterprise would meet it; under this logic, slaveholders were merely "agents" of consumers, with consumers (rather than workers) "the primary bulwark of free labor."[33] Although the realm of the political in this instance is limited to the marketplace, consumer activism in the nineteenth century was not about validating capitalism.[34]

By contrast, Made in the Free World understands the market as a tool for social change, but not one focused on tempering capitalism. Rather, ethical consumption in this iteration is the means through which capitalism can actually be bolstered, aided by digital media and a brand culture that can harvest value from seeming ethical. For example, in June 2014, Made in a Free World announced another partnership between the U.S. State Department and the nonprofit: the fall 2014 release of FRDM™ (Forced Labor Risk Determination and Mitigation, or FREEDOM). This "revolutionary software product," aimed at businesses, claims that it "will provide companies with a clear blueprint to mitigate their risk of unknowingly investing in suppliers who exploit forced or child labor. This strategic downward pressure on a supply chain has the power to disrupt illicit networks and empower vulnerable populations with freedom."[35] The means to "remediate risk" are vague: "strengthening vendor agreements," "policy improvements," "industry best practices," and, the most specific, "access to a network of vetted suppliers." To promote the product, Made in a Free World draws attention to the potential increased value for corporations: "More than ever, consumers align their purchasing power with companies who share their values. Our goal is to enable businesses to meet this demand without negatively affecting bottom lines. By strategically investing in [Made in a Free World] suppliers, when necessary, companies will become the new leaders of the free world."[36] Through the use of algorithms and digital platforms, FRDM conveys that one can abolish slavery while also making a profit and strengthening the market overall.

With companies as the putatively new leaders of the "free world," the site's complicity with neoliberal racial capitalism is clear, as is the line they draw between slavery and capitalism. *Freedom* here means a trickle-down logic of corporate freedom, where corporations set the terms. Further, by using the term *risk*, Made in a Free World and FRDM participate in neoliberal ideals of securitization and risk management. The concerns about slavery and labor are first and foremost a threat to the bottom line in an era where an ethical consumer is a profitable one. This is made especially plain in a letter from Made in a Free World to companies, urging them to sign up: "Many companies are quickly joining the FRDM˙ network and seeing the benefits in their bottom line. As you know, high consumer confidence = more profit for your business!"[37] Since 2014, FRDM has been given a more central role in the organization's aims. Those who take the Slavery Footprint survey are encouraged to write letters to their favorite companies urging them to use FRDM in order to "bankrupt slavery." Consumers can take this a step further through their purchases, as noted on Made in a Free World company websites: "The best way to support freedom in supply chains is to shop from Made In A Free World companies!" Part of what makes contemporary capitalist ethical consumption so problematic is the creation of value through poverty and environmental degradation, and their supposed amelioration through consumption. By claiming to investigate their supply chains through the use of digital platforms, companies are given a means to strengthen their brands via appeals to consumers concerned about labor practices.

Through the use of algorithms to supposedly uncover forced labor in a supply chain, Made in a Free World reinforces the notion that data can solve complex issues, a discourse echoed by Justin Dillon: "We live in a digitally connected and data-driven economy. We have the tools and information needed to uncover slavery and end it."[38] Dillon anticipates future partnerships that include companies with "expertise in data mining and predictive analytics" to further Made in a Free World's capabilities, including a collaboration with SAP (what Dillon calls "a Facebook for business—connecting more than 1.7 million companies in over 190 countries") to increase capacity.[39] Big data and digital technologies are therefore the solutions to what gets constituted as a problem of opacity. In other words, variables like race and migration become externalities to the algorithm, and gross asymmetries in global power are obfuscated by an emphasis on consumer sovereignty. FRDM uses a "global slavery database" built by mathematician Mira Bernstein, who collected data on "where slavery is most prevalent and what products it affects." From there, Bernstein created an algorithm that relies on just three factors to determine slavery and its presence in a supply chain. At present, FRDM does not account for "other risk factors that could indicate a prevalence of slave labor like, for instance, migration data," but the goal is to include that in the future. There is nothing about race, white supremacy, or migration.[40]

This combination of algorithmic governance, ethical consumption, and brand culture is bound up with Made in a Free World's postracial fantasy. Whereas algorithmic governance de-emphasizes the affective in favor of supposed emotional neutrality, Slavery Footprint and FRDM use affective reward as a point of entry into participation, where feeling ethical (and thus good) is emphasized over feeling guilt. Feeling ethical here is articulated to whiteness in a manner similar to green consumption's whiteness.[41] Julie Guthman details how with alternative food systems in particular, whiteness is reproduced in part through the colorblind rhetoric of "if they only knew," a phrase prevalent in alternative food movements that presumes that if only people were made aware of the food system's injustice, then changing to a supposedly better system would naturally follow.[42] Beyond erasing both racism and difference, there is little to no consideration of whiteness and universalism, including the belief that whiteness's values are "widely shared."[43] By consuming the right things, ethical neoliberal consumer-citizens can construct themselves as outside of power, as innocent, as pure; this is inextricable from both white comfort and denial.

Such an emphasis on moral purity (and thus superiority) contributed to the critique of the free produce movement made by abolitionists skeptical about what they viewed as the movement's fixation on individual moral purity instead of abolishing slavery. Further, these abolitionists emphasized the futility of attempting to disentangle oneself from slavery, which "interpenetrated every aspect of American life and, indeed, the world economy."[44] For them, attempting to eradicate slavery without using slave-made products would mean eschewing the use of goods like paper, an obvious necessity for abolitionist newspapers. The totality of the system meant that it would be impossible to act without engaging in some way the effects of slavery; as such, rather than a politics of purity centered on consumption, abolitionists critical of the free produce movement recognized their own implication within the system and organized from there. Critics also noted that the "line between free and slave labor was fuzzier than the free producers assumed."[45]

Yet if the blurriness of free and slave labor was a consideration for free produce advocates, it is unthought for Slavery Footprint and Made in a Free World. FRDM's very existence is premised on the assumption that companies and brands are unaware of the conditions of production along the supply chain. Slavery Footprint suggests that "knowing" is "not hard for [the brands]" despite the fact that the brands' presumed innocence relies on the supposed complexity of the supply chain.[46] By claiming that it is "not hard for them" to identify the use of forced labor within the supply chain, Slavery Footprint solidifies a division between free and forced labor, wherein unfree labor would be knowable if only the brands would try. The site rests on a contradiction, then: the consumer is implicated as the prompt for brands—as if all they need is for consumers to ask—thereby rendering the consumer culpable; but simultaneously, Slavery Footprint actively de-emphasizes feeling guilty and, in fact, instructs users not to feel it. Like the free produce activists who could not imagine a politics outside of the market, the site views consumers as agents of change with respect to the market and presumes that they have enormous power over brands. There is no rejection of capitalism as a mode of production; as the site states, "A free market should come from free people." According to this logic, what does a "free" person look like? What is "free" labor under capitalism?

Freedom/Slavery and Labor

One of Slavery Footprint's central assumptions is that there is a firm distinction between free and unfree labor, and that the latter is merely an aberration within a capitalist mode of production that otherwise works well. Drawing on a familiar narrative about U.S. chattel slavery, the site, which was released on the 149th anniversary of the Emancipation Proclamation, argues that "one of the great triumphs of our world has been our ability to end such evil practices. People rose up against slavery and didn't mince words. 'Abolition' leaves no room for compromise." On the next click, in bold red letters: "Emancipation set the slaves free." Immediately following, the site notes, "That's what we like to think anyway. Yeah, we've heard there are still questionable work conditions. Sweatshops and the like. But buying, selling, and trafficking human beings? If that's happening, it must just be in wildly different cultures far from my influence. . . . Actually, no. That smart phone. That t-shirt, computer, cup of coffee . . . that's stuff we buy, and that's stuff that comes from slaves." This downplaying of "sweatshops and the like" as compared to "buying, selling, and trafficking human beings" reinforces a hierarchy of the tolerable by following it with an imagined response from the reader: "'But they're reputable brands! If they were running sweatshops, Oprah would be all over it.' True, but it's not that simple. The fact of the matter is, these reputable brands that we know and love, they just don't know where all the materials come from."[47] The site presumes that sweatshop labor is acknowledged and actively part of popular discourse—that someone like Oprah would be leading the charge against it—and promulgates the myth that companies are somehow innocent, unaware of their conscious decisions to exploit laborers and work environments constituted and worsened by deregulation and free trade agreements.

By using the abolition of U.S. chattel slavery as a way of creating shock value (that is, the shock a reader might feel that slavery is not, in fact, abolished), the site erases the persistence of slavery as a salient issue in the contemporary United States, one that implicates the biopolitics of everyday life.[48] The terms *slavery* and *slave traders* provide gravity and moral import while simultaneously expunging the afterlife of slavery, a maneuver that is prevalent within the larger antitrafficking movement. Drawing on Toni Morrison, Tryon Woods identifies this as the deployment of "the specter of African slaves as 'surrogate selves' through which to meditate on the ongoing problems of human freedom global capitalism still presents."[49] Through ahistoricism and what Woods observes as anti-Blackness, the antitrafficking movement—of which Slavery Footprint is a part—uses Black suffering and Black struggle, though as Woods notes, not out of solidarity "with actually existing black communities."[50] In the case of Slavery Footprint, this Black suffering becomes a part of the brand Made in a Free World and is central to the construction of an ethical consumer-citizen who is also an "abolitionist." Whiteness is produced in this use of Black suffering to constitute an ethical subject who rescues an other from the Global South. Yet it is crucial here to also acknowledge the relief of feeling ethical in the face of staggering global inequality, including within the United States. In other words, supposed emotionally neutral tools like the algorithms used by Made in a Free World assuage white guilt while pointing to an increasingly data-driven future capable of rendering race irrelevant, or at least the effects of racial inequality more opaque. FRDM's purportedly defetishizing algorithm reifies a postrace discourse: the algorithm will reveal slave labor in the supply chain while simultaneously obfuscating and erasing the racialized power dynamics inherent in global labor configurations.

Framing "modern-day slavery" as worse than U.S. chattel slavery is widespread within the antitrafficking movement and is apparent in Made in a Free World's argument that there are "more slaves today than at any time in human history."[51] This echoes movement leader Kevin Bales, author of *Disposable People: New Slavery in the Global Economy,* who claims that there "are more slaves alive today than all the people stolen from Africa in the time of the transatlantic slave trade."[52] Once again, chattel slavery is used as a foil for what Bales considers "real" slavery. Woods writes, "For Bales, in the 'new' or 'real' slavery, 'race means very little': 'The criteria of enslavement today . . . do not concern color, tribe, or religion; they focus on weakness, gullibility, and deprivation.'"[53] Using language similar to Slavery Footprint, Bales evacuates race from the discussion, while replacing U.S. chattel slavery (and any discussion of reparations, at a minimum) in the process. The effort to supplant or elide the specificity of U.S. chattel slavery in favor of attending to modern-day slavery is not unique to the antitrafficking movement, as evidenced by an interactive program promising an embodied experience of the antebellum United States. A paradigmatic example, the Follow the North Star Experience at the Conner Prairie Historic Park in Fishers, Indiana, was an eighteen-year program that placed participants in the roles of enslaved people attempting escape along the Underground Railroad. According to Conner Prairie's vice president and CEO Cathryn Ferree, the park sought to offer an "educational experience that would make people feel empathetic, but not personally victimized, in learning about slavery."[54] In addition to critiques that the program traumatized Black participants—including students as young as twelve—scholars and others underscored how the program erased slavery's ongoing effects into the present. At the end of the program, participants were told that they should assess their Slavery Footprint in order to challenge slavery in the present.[55]

On Slavery Footprint's website, the coercion behind supposedly free labor is masked by the site's reliance on slavery to shore up the false division between free and coerced labor. This distinction is evident in the site's belief in creating the new brand—Made in a Free World—that would source products from supposedly non-forced labor. There is no mention of what this type of labor might look like (would sweatshop labor be considered non-forced labor?), nor is there any acknowledgment that capitalism as a mode of production necessitates exploitation for the extraction of surplus value.[56] As many scholars of race and slavery argue, the postemancipation era reconfigured life for ex-slaves into what could hardly be considered "freedom."[57] Saidiya Hartman's work in particular alters the grammar of *freedom* by revealing the reconceptualization of Black freedom as indebtedness within a framework of freedom and emancipation. Reconceptualizing Black freedom as indebtedness obscures the subjugation and domination engendered by a discourse of rights.[58] Instead of a pure break from slavery into freedom, Hartman emphasizes the continued entanglement of freedom and bondage postemancipation.

If the line between free and unfree is indistinct under capitalism, the site's use of the word *slavery* becomes similarly open to question. Part of the difficulty in making sense of what is (or is not) slavery is that for Marx, all labor is coerced within capitalism. What, then, is the definition of a slave? Slavery Footprint offers an explanation buried in the methodology section of the site:

How do we define Slavery (Forced Labor)?
Anyone who is forced to work without pay, being economically exploited, and is unable to walk away. Note: Forced Labor, also known as involuntary servitude, may result when unscrupulous employers exploit workers made more vulnerable by high rates of unemployment, poverty, crime, discrimination, corruption, political conflict, or cultural acceptance of the practice. Immigrants are particularly vulnerable, but individuals also may be forced into labor in their own countries. Female victims of forced or bonded labor,

especially women and girls in domestic servitude, are often sexually exploited as well.[59]

The header's elision of peculiarities through the use of the parenthetical—slavery is akin to forced labor—extends throughout the definition, where forced labor is a synonym for slavery, which is a synonym for involuntary servitude. Such distinctions are important in part because they are central to understanding racial formation and processes of racialization and their associated hierarchies of value. This vague definition, by contrast, does not center the transformation of a person into a commodity or attend at all to race. Rather, Slavery Footprint's description of what the site terms *slavery* blames "unscrupulous" employers and poverty but leaves unexamined the ways that racial capitalism, heteropatriarchy, and imperialism render certain populations "vulnerable" to poverty, crime, discrimination, and even the effects of climate change. Exploitation is relegated to the realm of "forced" labor; instead of viewing exploitation as foundational for capitalism, the site renders it a deviation wrought by greedy employers. Marx's crucial point is made plain here: there is coercion behind both forms of labor, but this coercion—force—is articulated on the body in different ways (and regarding slavery, through overt violence), and the modalities of the coercion are very different. Slavery Footprint ignores this coercion behind putatively free labor and presumes that free labor constitutes a space of freedom.

Moreover, as Marx shows, capital had to develop systems of coercion that could convince people of their freedom (e.g., juridical freedom), an arguably more effective system in that by operating at a more subjective level, this type of coercion is disguised as noncoercion. The centrality of freedom in many accounts of early U.S. history, particularly in relation to the emergence of democracy and capitalism, elides the profound unfreedom for the many upon which freedom for some hinged. This erases the ways that wage labor is ultimately reliant on constraint and coercion as opposed to choice and consent, as claimed by liberalism.[60] Further, the system of slavery worked to legitimate wage labor by virtue of the fact that wage laborers were ostensibly free and could therefore be considered indicators of liberal progress. The idea of not being a slave via one's whiteness (and thus able to receive the "wages of whiteness"[61]) was sufficient to satisfy problematic labor relations with respect to wage labor: "If the satisfaction of not being a slave was enough to smooth white workers' entrance into wage relations, then slavery—simply as a negative referent—becomes essential to the development of American capitalism."[62]

Through their reliance on algorithms and data to uncover what they term "slavery," Made in a Free World promulgates the notion of the digital as not only neutral and separate from race and capitalism but as the ideal solution precisely because the technology obscures race. Within a context of neoliberal poverty management and consumer activism, Slavery Footprint produces a form of ethical subjectivity that thinks about, and acts against, racialized labor arrangements (which are never named as such) through consumption and digital media rather than emotion. Situating its users as modern-day abolitionists and rescuers, Slavery Footprint works to constitute an ethical consumer-citizen who consumes a social good that liberates a racialized other elsewhere. In a 2012 speech on modern-day slavery at the Clinton Global Initiative, then president Barack Obama emphasized:

> Every citizen can take action: by learning more; by going to the website that we helped create—SlaveryFootprint.org; by speaking up and insisting that the clothes we wear, the food we eat, the products we buy are made free of forced labor; by standing up against the degradation and abuse of women. That's how real change happens—from the bottom up.[63]

This entanglement of ethical consumption and citizenship is further complicated by the racial dynamics at play in these affective appeals that circulate through digital media. Stitching ethical subjectivity into algorithmic governance bolsters technological fetishism, a discourse that is especially salient in light of the call for more technology—body and dash cameras, predictive analytics—to combat police violence against racialized communities and populations.

Moreover, this ethical subject is not divorced from a broader social media culture of virtue signaling, white wokeness, and performative antiracism wherein feeling enlightened and woke (and presenting that through digital media) obscures other actions. Data and algorithms are key sites for the production of race—not just reifying existing racial formations but modifying and constituting them as well. Critically, the ongoing datafication of race and racialized bodies constitutes a new racial formation in the twenty-first century, one that attempts to transcend emotion.

Refusing Prescription

Kara Walker and Black Feminist Cultural Production

*All the violence and killing that colored people have suffered
since Freedom may just be a drop in the bucket to what they
put on us in slavery time, but God only knows what it will be
in the future.*

—Margaret Walker, *Jubilee*

*I do what I'm feeling and what I'm feeling is monstrous. And
I do it in the nicest possible way.*

—Kara Walker, "The Un-Private Collection:
Kara Walker and Ava DuVernay"

In 2007, the Walker Art Center in Minneapolis, Minnesota, held a
retrospective of Kara Walker's work, which was the "first full-scale
American museum survey" of her oeuvre.[1] To celebrate the opening
of the exhibition—*Kara Walker: My Complement, My Enemy, My Oppressor, My Love*—the Walker hosted an after-hours party with drinks
and hors d'oeuvres, where museum members and others could have
an early glimpse of Walker's large-scale cut-paper silhouettes before
the exhibition officially opened. People sipped "Targetinis" as they
chatted and meandered through the galleries, drinking in images of
sexual violence and the sexual economy central to chattel slavery.[2]
Given that it was prior to the selfie/Instagram era, there were few
phones out in the museum, but the predominantly white audience
joked, laughed, and made merry, downing bright red cocktails while
moving in and among Kara Walker's staggering pieces. Seven years
later, Walker made viewer response to her work the focus of the aptly

titled film *An Audience*, which documents audience reaction to the
last hour of *A Subtlety*, a thirty-five-foot-tall sphinx made out of Styrofoam and covered in sugar in the former Domino Sugar plant in
Brooklyn, New York. Walker, in other words, is not shocked by how
her work is taken up and engaged with by audiences. Rather, as *An
Audience* suggests, Walker anticipated the often grotesque and vulgar responses to her pieces, highlighting what happens at the intersections of visual culture and whiteness with respect to art depicting
histories of racialized sexual violence, conquest, and commodity
culture.[3]

Margaret Walker's *Jubilee* also challenges the hegemonic
constructions and uses of the history of U.S. chattel slavery. Such
contestation was often concurrent with the cultural productions
given mainstream attention. Margaret Walker wrote *Jubilee* in 1966,
centering the life of formerly enslaved woman Vyry as the novel
moves from the antebellum era through Reconstruction. In 1977,
Walker sued Alex Haley for plagiarism, claiming that "fifteen scenes
from *Jubilee* showed up in *Roots*."[4] Yet Haley's masculinist narrative
garnered widespread success while Walker's was obscured. In 1960,
playwright Lorraine Hansberry wrote *The Drinking Gourd*, a television screenplay about slavery that NBC refused to air, calling it too
"much of a hot potato."[5] Said producer Dore Schary in a 1960 interview with the *New York Herald Tribune*, "'NBC indicated to me that
it was difficult to find sponsors willing to go along with a frank ex-
ploration of the background of the Civil War. Even when you strive
for an honest, objective presentation of old controversy, there are
bound to be people offended.'"[6] *The Drinking Gourd* was critiqued as
"too strong for general viewing," but as Robert Nemiroff, executor of
Hansberry's estate, later wrote to the chair of NBC, "it was because
of something subtler and ultimately more disquieting: Hansberry's
treatment of what the system did to the whites."[7] Margaret Walker's
and Hansberry's respective artistic engagements with chattel slavery
were sidelined in favor of a triumphant and masculinist narrative as
seen in *Roots*.

Racial formation is inextricable from the production of emotion,
made particularly potent through mediating the history of U.S. chattel slavery. Mainstream media about the history of slavery generate
feelings that turn what is constituted as the problem of race into a

safe racial orientation—for example, encouraging Black viewers of *Roots* to shift anger into pride. This disciplinary impetus is driven in part by form, with an educational video game emphasizing interactivity as opposed to 1960s television documentaries, which relied on the seriousness of the genre to construct whiteness as rational. The media environment of a particular era, along with how racial formation operates in specific historical and cultural contexts, means that different media forms are more effective in guiding affective governance and, specifically, teaching people how to feel about race. In the twenty-first century, racial formation is increasingly shaped by algorithmic governance. But instead of a technologically deterministic argument, or one that attends primarily to formal concerns, *Media and the Affective Life of Slavery* emphasizes the role that media culture and its extensions play in producing and managing emotions that contribute to racial formation.

Scholars and writers like Toni Morrison, Toni Cade Bambara, and Margaret Walker were retheorizing and reimagining the history of U.S. chattel slavery through a Black feminist lens at the same time that *Roots* became a focal point for issues of race and the legacies of slavery in the United States. Here, I focus on Kara Walker's *An Audience* as part of this broader corpus of Black feminist cultural production that counters dominant uses of the history of slavery to shape emotion.[8] Walker's piece features a complex examination of whiteness and white supremacy, akin to Hansberry's *The Drinking Gourd*, which underscored a different threat to whiteness (and thus was one of the reasons that the screenplay was never filmed or aired): how white supremacy destroys white people too—albeit in different ways—by virtue of its soul-killing nature. As Hansberry's compatriot and friend James Baldwin writes, "People pay for what they do, and still more for what they allowed themselves to become. And they pay for it very simply by the lives they lead. The crucial thing, here, is that the sum of these individual abdications menaces life all over the world."[9] Hansberry offers a condemnation of white supremacy that includes all of its devastations. Similarly, with *An Audience*, Walker highlights the adaptability of whiteness to antiracist critique alongside a refusal to prescribe and discipline feeling.

Indeed, Walker offers a denunciation of white supremacy and whiteness that shows how whiteness desires and uses Blackness to constitute itself. As with Hansberry, Walker also attends to how this is a devastating ideology and set of power relations, one that ravages everyone, though of course in critically different ways. Whereas texts like *Flight to Freedom* and the 1960s TV documentaries constitute Blackness through how it is imagined by whiteness, especially with respect to emotion, there is no acknowledgment of white supremacy, much less as a logic that has implications for white people too. Whiteness is thus able to remain slippery and invisibilized even as it is simultaneously hypervisible. Much like Dungey and Hansberry, Walker challenges authoritative histories and dominant notions of time that so often uphold and erase racial violence, both banal and spectacular. As Rod Ferguson reminds us, "To remember the past, we must act against the storm of progress."[10] I turn now to Walker's work that upends linearity by revealing the layers of palimpsestic space, made visible in ongoing racialized and gendered labor dynamics.

A Subtlety and An Audience

Walker's installation *At the behest of Creative Time Kara E. Walker has confected: A Subtlety, or the "Marvelous Sugar Baby," an Homage to the unpaid and overworked Artisans who have refined our Sweet tastes from the cane fields to the Kitchens of the New World on the Occasion of the demolition of the Domino Sugar Refining Plant* was commissioned to mark the demolition of the Domino Sugar Factory during July 2014.[11] The piece was composed of the enormous "sugar baby" sphinx and fifteen sculptures of brown children, some cast in resin and coated with molasses and sugar, and others cast in sugar; by the end of the exhibition, the three made entirely of sugar "had collapsed and mostly melted away."[12] Coated in white sugar, the sphinx rendered visible the racial stereotypes, contradictions, and constructions of Black femininity underpinning histories of slavery, sugar production, and racialized and gendered labor. Walker built the sphinx primarily from Styrofoam and gave her a "Mammy head kerchief and exaggerated the nose and lips. . . . Walker also endowed her with buxom breasts, sensual curves, a positively giant rear end, and a ten-foot vulva."[13] The material construction of racial spectacle embodied by the piece makes explicit the conflicting forms of desire that, as Glenda Carpio suggests, also fueled minstrelsy, which Carpio offers as a key framework for understanding Walker's installation. Similar to minstrelsy, the "very act of viewing" *A Subtlety* was made "subject to the gaze of others," particularly in the afterlife of the piece made possible via the *Digital Sugar Baby*, which encouraged the forms of interactivity and user participation so familiar to life in the digital age: hashtagging, sharing photos, and even a digital guest book of viewers' experiences of the work gave *A Subtlety* a kind of "permanency denied it by its physical destruction."[14] Walker underscores the underlying power dynamics and racialized fantasies, desires, consumption, and terror that undergird both minstrelsy and chattel slavery.[15] Critically, Walker demonstrates how whiteness—made spectacularly visible through the shining white sugar "skin" of the sphinx—"as an identity, a set of ideologies . . . constructs distorted notions of Blackness."[16] Yet, similar to what I have shown throughout *Media and the Affective Life of Slavery*, the sphinx also points to how whiteness relies on fantasies of Blackness to construct whiteness.

My focus here is not *A Subtlety*, however, but rather the piece that Walker made after the sculpture was demolished: *An Audience*. During the last hour of the final day of the exhibition, six people with cameras were present to "capture whatever happened" among viewers. As Walker notes in the wall didactic accompanying *An Audience*, the camerapeople were instructed to "record the waning spectacle but also to observe the audience in the act of looking—at the work, at themselves, at one another, and especially looking at their phones and cameras. During the last few minutes of the exhibition viewers were invited to touch the sugar baby—to have an unmediated experience with the object."[17] Walker then edited and produced the footage into a twenty-seven-minute work.

In contrast to study guides, lesson plans, 1960s documentaries, and educational video games, Walker is not interested in shaping behavior or prompting a particular emotional reaction. The idea of spectacle invokes histories of racialized subjection, certainly, along with the carnivalesque, a show, a curiosity. What *An Audience* captures is a scene of layered complexity and Walker's keen understanding of the intersections between contemporary media culture, racial formation, and representation. Walker does not expressly discipline patron interaction but lets it unfold within this broader context of self-mediation, race, gentrification, and the ongoing legacies of chattel slavery. During the opening of *An Audience,* the viewer sees a sign at the entrance promoting the digital circulation of audience engagement with the exhibition: "Please do not touch the artwork but do share pictures on social media with #KaraWalkerDomino." Audiences were thus invited to engage this history in a way that makes clear its continuation into the present—namely, through the increasingly pervasive form of social media. In this way, Walker contributes to a broader conversation about the digital circulation of images of Black death and racialized violence, wherein clips of police violence and terror against Black bodies loop endlessly in the digital realm, quotidian violence that becomes part of the iconography of everyday life through the digital economy.[18] The digital uptake of *A Subtlety* through photos—selfies and otherwise—with the piece generated buzz for the exhibition, certainly, but also underscored how the ceaseless flow of networked imagery makes continuous what is otherwise ephemeral.

An Audience begins with a medium-long shot of the sphinx's face; the viewer sees people milling about, fanning themselves, alternately gazing at their phones and the sculpture. It quickly cuts to a shot of people entering and leaving the space, framed by the vivid green weeds surrounding the pathway, demarcating the site as an industrial one. A white woman enters pushing a baby stroller, accompanied by a young, white child. She audibly exclaims "Wow" in a tone presumably meant to indicate amazement and wonder to the child. Behind her, a Black woman enters and covers her mouth in shock. The camera zooms in for a close-up, highlighting the woman's fist blocking her mouth. She shakes her head in dismay as she takes in the piece, puts her hand over her heart, and pats herself as she walks closer to the sculpture. Within the first few minutes of the film, we see audience reaction divided along a Black/white color line, yet Walker does not discipline response.[19] Although the juxtaposition between the two women's initial reactions is stark, Walker is not shaming—the camera does not, for instance, follow the white woman and monitor the rest of her experience with the exhibition, nor are explicitly vulgar engagements edited so as to be contrasted with ostensibly better interactions with the work.

Approximately five minutes in, the viewer sees a young Black boy posing with the melting sugar baby, smiling for the camera, looking at his mother. We see this same child throughout *An Audience,* at the very beginning as he enters the space and toward the end of the piece when the camera follows him as he approaches the sphinx. He is in the center of the frame, turned slightly toward a white woman with a satchel who is leaning forward to touch the piece, her shadow reflecting on the body of the sphinx so that it is almost as if she is touching her reflection. He is tiny compared to the sphinx, and the gleaming whiteness of the sugar is glaring. Children reappear often throughout *An Audience,* offering their own unfiltered commentary

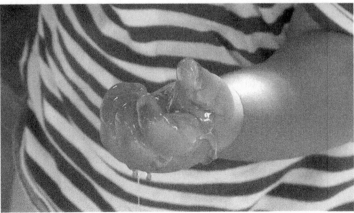

Children feature prominently in An Audience. *Kara Walker,* An Audience, *2014. Digital video with sound, 27:18 minutes. Artwork copyright Kara Walker; courtesy of Sikkema Jenkins & Co., New York.*

on the work. At one point, a small Black child asks, "What is that smell? It smells nasty," while his younger sister grimaces in agreement. Another child of color—a toddler—is gently reprimanded by his mother and her friends who laugh in dismay when he puts his hand in the sticky melted sugar on the ground and begins to lick it off. Such unself-conscious interaction with Walker's work throws the adult reactions into sharp relief: the adults we see posing often look sheepish or awkward while they wait for their friends or partners to snap their photo. Some, certainly, are brazen as they pose in lewd and violent ways, reaching their arms up as though they are touching the sphinx's nipples or pretending to cup the buttocks. But there is often a sense of defaulting into expected reactions. In contrast, the children are asked by their parents or caregivers to stand next to the work, to smile, to look at the camera, to pose—their otherwise unfiltered affective reactions are not containable within the different frames of racial feeling and behavior inhabited by the adults. By showing this range of response that spans from violent and vulgar to woke and reverent—but that is not divided along clear racial lines—Walker subverts our expectations about who will behave or respond in what ways.

"I Was Spying"

Given that so much of the piece emphasizes the practices of self-mediation, *An Audience* offers us a way to think through the entanglement of racial formation, media culture, affect, and histories of slavery in the digital age. Much like *A Subtlety,* Walker's *An Audience* invokes complex histories, adding an additional layer of mediation via film. *An Audience* has a surveillant feel, with Walker herself noting, "I was spying." Yet, Walker's surveillant gaze and both *A Subtlety* and *An Audience* do not suggest a correct way to view or engage with the work or how one should feel while in the exhibition space. Rather than policing reaction, *An Audience* makes possible larger questions, including what particular behavior suggests about contemporary racial formation, racialized subjectivity, gender, and violence. This is not to say that *An Audience* or even Walker herself is agnostic with respect to violent or degrading responses. Rather, she is unsurprised, as she discusses in an interview:

I put a giant 10-foot vagina in the world and people respond to giant 10-foot vaginas in the way that they do. It's not unexpected. Maybe I'm sick. . . . Human behavior is so mucky and violent and messed-up and inappropriate. And I think my work draws on that. It comes from there. It comes from responding to situations like that, and it pulls it out of an audience. I've got a lot of video footage of that [behavior].[20]

But contrary to the texts I have discussed throughout *Media and the Affective Life of Slavery*, there is no right way that presumes it is outside of power. In other words, Walker demonstrates that the violence of these histories and their reach into the present is complex and layered in ways that are not reducible to innocence or feeling the supposedly correct feelings. Walker is thus simultaneously critiquing the notion of prescription, which narrows the possibilities of art to expand our imaginations—political and otherwise—to a very specific range.

As such, *An Audience* also offers an implicit commentary on whiteness, wokeness, and digital media. The social media display of wokeness renders antiracism into a performance inextricable from the demands of the attention economy. Posting to highlight one's self-awareness with respect to, for instance, race and white privilege is stitched into the logics of self-branding and visibility—that is, wokeness in this sense requires being seen as antiracist and is affirmed and rewarded with social media attention. Walker, by contrast, suggests messiness and contradiction, an acknowledgment of the enduring and adaptive forms of whiteness and white supremacy over the centuries. As the arc of Walker's oeuvre has made clear, she is not interested in prescription. Rather, she makes explicit that there is no correct way to feel or to engage, and the presumption that one exists in effect diminishes the enormity of this violence and the complexity of these histories. Instead, the work asks the viewer to consider what is made visible and what remains hidden and unknowable, what is not captured through mediation and what is lost in the containment of algorithmic representation. The emphasis on unknowability challenges masculinist ideas of mastery, knowing, permanence, and certainty. The "right" way does not exist because to suggest as much is to already trap, contain, and discipline that which is unruly, messy, complicated, and unknowable precisely because of the enormity of violence, which includes the violence of the archive.[21] To discipline reaction is to enter into the presumption of mastery and containability of emotion, which exceeds and escapes attempts to shape it. Further, Walker emphasizes the layers of history and an understanding of time that is not a progressive telos. The ephemeral nature of A Subtlety highlights and confronts notions of permanence, particularly through erecting a sculpture meant for eternity. Walker refuses this, instead producing a piece meant to be destroyed, from materials both long-lasting (Styrofoam) and evanescent (sugar). The form—sculpture—and the piece itself challenge the presumptions of hegemonic renderings of history, especially in relation to U.S. chattel slavery and its afterlives. Walker's work highlights the relationality of the racial formations of Blackness and whiteness and the ways that racism is a "cannibalistic force" that "suffuses all social relations to the point where racists and their victims consume each other and themselves."[22] Both A Subtlety and An Audience offer a meditation on consumption—metaphorical and literal (in the form of sugar consumption)—as one of the ways that slavery's legacies continue to shape the present. At the very end of An Audience, the viewer sees the destruction of the sphinx, set to the jubilant "España, Rhapsody for Orchestra" by nineteenth-century French composer Emmanuel Chabrier. The music is, indeed, rhapsodic and triumphant as sugar sprays while Styrofoam chunks of the sculpture are trucked away. There is something akin to ecstasy in the demolition, in the impermanence.

Rather than policing reaction and promulgating respectability politics, Walker's work prompts a different set of questions not focused solely on supposedly correct viewer engagement. How do audiences engage with Black feminist creativity and cultural production, and what does this reveal about contemporary racial formation and racialized subjectivity? This is not to suggest a relativist position (and to erase critiques of individual behavior), but rather it is clear that Walker is more interested in the contours of the discourse that her work generates. As the wall didactic accompanying An Audience clarified, A Subtlety became "a talking point about historic injustice, artistic hubris, the public gaze, responsible viewership, black audiences vs. white ones, black female representation, aggressive male behavior, self recognition, and 'selfies.'"[23] For the last hour of the last day of *A Subtlety*, patrons were encouraged to interact with the piece and were invited to touch it. This form of immersion does not promise that one will "become a slave," or that the experience is akin to "living history," but instead asks viewers to engage this history in a way that makes clear its continuations into the present. We watch people's haptic engagement with the piece, their hands gliding over the "skin" of the sphinx, touching the nipples, feeling the stickiness. *An Audience* includes several close-ups of patrons' struggle to move through the melted sugar: flip flops and sandals are peeled away from feet as the heat of the Brooklyn summer makes the work even more sensory. Even this interactivity implicates the viewer. Walker sought discomfort, which is messy and incomplete and, perhaps most importantly, not readily resolved; she implicates her audience throughout her work but especially in this piece, where "participation was transformed into a kind of complicity."[24] In so doing, Walker does not reproduce what Saidiya Hartman calls the "slipperiness of empathy." For Hartman, the projection of self onto the other "in order to better understand the other" results in an elision whereby the self is recentered: in making the "other's suffering one's own, this suffering is occluded by the other's obliteration."[25]

An Audience prompts us to consider what it means to teach someone how to feel about atrocity that is unrepresentable and to examine what this suggests about how we come to understand ourselves as racialized subjects. Walker's work does not presume how her audience will feel, nor does she seek to discipline it. Yet the title of the work—with the indefinite article preceding audience—suggests that this will continue. It is not *the* audience but *an* audience. It is one among many, not a specific, singular one. In this way, the role of media culture in producing and disciplining emotion will also continue, as changing racial formations require the cultivation of particular emotions. In the contemporary era, social media wokeness and feeling antiracist are dominant formations but go hand in hand with the proliferation of hypervisible (and state-sanctioned) white rage and its attendant white supremacist violence.

An Audience includes several close-ups of viewer engagement with the materiality of the work, with summer shoes getting caught in the melting sugar. Kara Walker, An Audience, 2014. Digital video with sound, 27:18 minutes. Artwork copyright Kara Walker; courtesy of Sikkema Jenkins & Co., New York.

This marks another way that slavery's afterlife persists, with whiteness continuing to shapeshift and extend old racial logics. Yet this exists alongside formations like Black Lives Matter that reveal and challenge slavery's residue. In describing Walker's overall body of work, Carpio suggests that through the difficulty in distinguishing "individual agents" among Walker's all-black cutouts, "she troubles the line between victims and perpetrators and renders visual how the toxicity of racism becomes part of a shared political unconscious that affects everyone, albeit in different registers."[26] Like Hansberry, Walker highlights how white supremacy ensnares everyone in its logics, though as Carpio emphasizes, this occurs asymmetrically, of course, with vastly different impacts. With *A Subtlety* and *An Audience*, Walker indicates how visual art has a purchase on the social too; in other words, it is not just popular culture that shapes the cultural imaginary. Here, Walker blurs the lines between the two, extending the exhibition space into the digital (and popular) realm.

The management of emotion continues to be a way of disciplining racialized populations, one that also works to shore up an ordered racial binary in the United States. The complexity of work like

Walker's points us to something much more generative than social media wokeness and its entanglement with the performative and its fixation on individual behavior.[27] There is no innocent positionality or correct feeling. *An Audience* pushes beyond the templates for racialized subjectivity that I have examined throughout *Media and the Affective Life of Slavery*. Instead of purity, Walker wants us to know that we have already touched the source.

Acknowledgments

The acknowledgments are one of my favorite places to begin when I open a book, and so for that reason I have been thinking about my own acknowledgments for about as long as I have been thinking about this project. Academia does not often provide many chances to publicly thank the enormous constellation of people who make intellectual work both possible and pleasurable, so I am grateful, in fact, to have this space to express my deep gratitude.

Thank you, first and foremost, to my incredible dissertation advisor, mentor, and friend Laurie Ouellette. Her shining brilliance, calm guidance, and ongoing support have been indispensable, and I am more thankful than I can express for the way that she exemplifies the best of an intellectual life and for how much she has shaped mine. I could not have done this without her and owe her my deepest thanks for her generosity, kindness, and encouragement. Thank you to the tremendous Roderick Ferguson for his unceasing mentorship and support. Among so much else, Rod taught me how to really read, to trust myself, and to focus on the writing process as a creative one. I am so grateful for the wisdom that he has shared with me over tea, and I deeply value his approach to academia. Thank you to Lisa Sun-Hee Park for her wonderful guidance and mentorship and for continuing to share her brilliance with me (sometimes over delicious dinners!). I treasure Lisa's insights, and I continue to reflect on all that she has taught me about how to approach a text and how to grapple with theoretical questions. Laurie, Rod, and Lisa have had a profound impact on my thinking and who I am as a person, and I am immensely grateful. In addition to being astonishing scholars and thinkers, they are outstanding teachers—their exemplary pedagogy informs and shapes my own teaching. It is a joy to know them and to learn from them.

I am fortunate to have had guidance from so many terrific mentors. I am grateful to Annie Hill for her mentorship and support as a member of my dissertation committee. Thank you to Cesare Casarino for productive conversations that informed chapter 4. Many thanks to the singular Regina Kunzel, whose support and guidance have been so generously given. Both Reg and Dara Strolovitch have been wonderful mentors and friends, and I am grateful for their presence in my life. Thank you to the amazing Kevin Murphy for his ongoing support and for introducing me to Laurie, for which I will always be thankful.

I am deeply grateful for the mentorship of Diane Negra, who generously read and commented on chapter 1 (in handwritten comments mailed from Europe) and who has supported my work over many years. My time with her in Dublin during February 2020 as a Discovery Institute fellow was the easy highlight of an otherwise immensely challenging year. It has been a joy and honor to collaborate with and learn from her. Her guidance and friendship mean so much to me.

It has been a dream to work with the University of Minnesota Press. Thank you to Danielle Kasprzak for believing in the project from the beginning. Working with the remarkable Leah Pennywark has been an utter delight. Leah has been a tremendous editor, generous with her time, and a steady, brilliant, and gracious guide through ideas, writing, and the book's process. I am beyond grateful to her for her assistance and support. Thank you also to Anne Carter and Jason Weidemann for their tireless work in shepherding this project.

I have benefited tremendously over the years from conferences and workshops, as well as colleagues who generously read and commented on drafts of my work and offered support. Thank you to Sarah Banet-Weiser, Herman Gray, and Josh Kun for their generative feedback at USC's Summer Institute on Diversity in Media and Culture. Sarah has continued to be a wonderful mentor and friend. Thank you also to Erica Ball, Paula Chakravartty, Jennifer DeClue, Jessyka Finley, Alicia Kozma, Kellie Moore, Amber Jamilla Musser, Britt Rusert, Tonia Sutherland, Jayne Swift, McKenzie Wark, and my grad school interlocutors, including Liz Ault, Karisa Butler-Wall, Tammy Cherelle Owens, Raechel Jolie, Rebecca Jurisz, Jasmine Mitchell, Helen Morgan Parmett, Ryan Murphy, Julie Wilson, and (Anne) Wolf.

Thank you to Sikkema Jenkins, especially Scott Briscoe, for granting me permission to view and work with Kara Walker's stunning *An Audience*. Thank you to Sona Basmadjian for her assistance with the David L. Wolper Collection at USC and the many archivists and librarians at the Schomburg Center for Research in Black Culture, including Cheryl Beredo, for helping me to find and sift through archival material.

Old Dominion University (ODU) has been a terrific place to land, and I am so thankful to be in a department of wonderful and supportive colleagues. Particular thanks to Alison Lietzenmayer (a rock!), Brittney Harris, Carla Harrell, and Brendan O'Hallarn. Before I began at ODU, I was told by several people who knew Avi Santo from afar that he would be an excellent colleague. He has been that and so much more, and I am deeply grateful for his steadfast guidance, encouragement, and mentorship. He is one of the smartest, most innovative, committed, and creative people I know, and I have learned an enormous amount from him. Thank you to my incredible students at ODU, especially Lily Kunda, Brittany Haslem, Megan Palko, Tiffany Daniel, Kayla Davis, Amber Edwards, Nick Arnold, and Claudia Garcia Mendoza. Danielle Goldstein was a brilliant and deeply kind student—she is profoundly missed. I have learned so much from and with Carmen Jones and am glad that we got to work together on a project before she began her PhD program. I am so thankful for my dear friend Myles McNutt, distiller of wisdom. He has been an amazing colleague, patient tennis coach, and my favorite power-walking companion who keeps me rich in baked goods and who never fails to make me laugh. Tim Anderson has been an enormously supportive and kind mentor and colleague. I am so grateful for his gentle guidance and generously given support. I am very thankful for my terrific comrade and friend Annemarie Navar-Gill. Liz Groeneveld is a great colleague and wonderful friend. Thank you to Kent Sandstrom for such kind and generous encouragement. I appreciate Andrea Battle-Coffer's joyful presence and ongoing support.

This book began as a dissertation in the company of Steve Dillon. I am grateful to him for his support, generosity, love, and encouragement during those years. I am also grateful to Michelle Verzal and the rest of the Dillon family for their love and support. One challenging but also wonderful aspect of academic life is living in many parts of the country. I am so grateful to have found amazing community in each place I have lived. Thank you to my Massachusetts friends Pooja Rangan, Josh Guilford, Jules Rosskam, Jina Kim, Lezlie Frye, Libby Sharrow, and (hilarious) Mara Toone. I am grateful to the people who made my transition to Norfolk easier and who were so warm and welcoming, including Vanessa Panfil, M.C. McDonald, Natalia Pilato, Caitlin Lynch, Liz Groeneveld, and Alison Reed. Two of my earlier teachers, Jan Smith and Rosemarie Scullion, taught me the deep pleasures of writing and thinking. I owe a great deal and deep thanks to Jane Stern, Amy Winters Champoux, and Jennifer Morgan. Thank you to my friends Megan Holm, Jay Foote, Linda Vieira, Adam Hauser, Owen Marciano, Andrea Flores, Matthew Pearson, Jaime and Jacob Wascalus, Conrad Carlozzi, and Caitlin Rogers. Khanisha Foster entered my life at the perfect moment; I am in awe over the magic she brings to the world and am grateful for her friendship. Ian and Kim Brannigan have been dear friends for many years and have supplied me with so many incredible meals and a lot of shared laughter. I am so deeply grateful for the wonderful and brilliant Jackie Arcy, a cherished friend and collaborator.

Thank you to my dearest friends Megan Kerman and Jon Grizzle, who have now left NYC for LA. This coast misses you. Aleksa Brown and I continue to marvel at our connection: Dear Sharon. I cannot believe that I get to know Cathie Cotten, Gerrard Norman, and now dearest Aliya, my Norfolk pack. Finding my beloved and brilliant Craig Agule has been the most unimaginable joy. His stellar copyediting made this a stronger book, and his love, support, and delicious meals sustained me through the final revision process. Perhaps at some point I will stop pinching myself.

The brilliant Marjorie Jolles has been an extraordinary teacher and dearest friend for more than fifteen years. My precious Laura Mason-Marshall, fount of joy and wisdom, means everything to me. Thank you to my oldest friend, Michael Landers, for being an incredible confidante and inspiration for more than thirty-two years. I do not have words to express my gratitude to Bernadine Mellis, Andrea Lawlor, Shugie Lawlor-Mellis, and Jordy Rosenberg, my cherished Northampton loves who saw me through an unexpectedly difficult time. Their laughter, kindness, joy, creativity, and wisdom mean so much to me. I cannot put into words my love and gratitude for

Gnome (de Guerre) Rosenberg. Being a "platonic coparent" with Jordy Rosenberg has been an immeasurable gift and profound joy that includes endless joking about our different (though symbiotic!) parenting styles.

My older brother Andrew has been immensely supportive from across the world, and I am very grateful for his love and encouragement—I feel his unyielding support from thousands of miles away. My parents, Carolyn and Joe, instilled in me a love of reading and a curiosity about the world that continues to shape me. I am very grateful for their ongoing belief in me and their interest in this project from its infancy, from my mom reading books about slavery to my dad asking me if they "get" to read my dissertation. Their excitement about this book means so much to me.

Brittany Farr has been a treasured and daily presence in my life since our chance meeting years ago. ("Best thing to come out of a conference.") She has read every single word of this book, in some cases several times over. I am beyond grateful for her love and friendship. FMOOC.

This book is for my younger brother Christopher, who has allowed me to call him "Munchie" for decades. I am so deeply grateful for him. His wisdom, love, support, hilarious sense of humor, and encouragement mean everything to me.

Notes

Introduction

1. Ask a Slave: The Web Series, "Ask a Slave Ep 1: Meet Lizzie Mae," September 1, 2013, YouTube video, 4:03, https://www.youtube.com/watch?v=X1IYH_MbJqA.

2. Ask a Slave: The Web Series, 7 years ago, comment on "Ask a Slave Ep 1."

3. Glenda Carpio, *Laughing Fit to Kill: Black Humor in the Fictions of Slavery* (New York: Oxford University Press, 2008), 13.

4. See, for example, Michelle Alexander's immensely popular book, *The New Jim Crow: Mass Incarceration in the Age of Colorblindness* (New York: New Press, 2012), which drew mainstream attention to slavery's legacy with respect to the U.S. carceral state.

5. See Christina Sharpe, *Monstrous Intimacies: Making Post-Slavery Subjects* (Durham, N.C.: Duke University Press, 2010); Jenny Sharpe, *Ghosts of Slavery: A Literary Archaeology of Black Women's Lives* (Minneapolis: University of Minnesota Press, 2003); and Kimberly Juanita Brown, *The Repeating Body: Slavery's Visual Resonance in the Contemporary* (Durham, N.C.: Duke University Press, 2015).

6. See Saidiya Hartman, *Lose Your Mother: A Journey along the Atlantic Slave Route* (New York: Farrar, Straus and Giroux, 2007); Christina Sharpe, *In the Wake: On Blackness and Being* (Durham, N.C.: Duke University Press, 2016); Michelle Commander, *Afro-Atlantic Flight: Speculative Returns and the Black Fantastic* (Durham, N.C.: Duke University Press, 2017); Brown, *Repeating Body*; and Alys Weinbaum, *The Afterlife of Reproductive Slavery: Biocapitalism and Black Feminism's Philosophy of History* (Durham, N.C.: Duke University Press, 2019).

7. Hartman, *Lose Your Mother*, 6.

8. Sara Ahmed, *The Cultural Politics of Emotion* (New York: Routledge, 2004), 40. Sharing similarities with both Brian Massumi and Sara Ahmed, Eric Shouse writes, "Feelings are *personal* and *biographical,* emotions are *social,* and affects are *prepersonal.*" "Feeling, Emotion, Affect," *M/C Journal* 8, no. 6 (2005): http://journal.media-culture.org.au/0512/03-shouse.php.

Although I appreciate Shouse's distinction, I do not separate affect and emotion in this chapter.

9. I am not focused on media or curricular materials that are explicitly conservative, like history textbooks produced for Texas that whitewash or altogether erase the history of slavery.

10. Avery Gordon, *Ghostly Matters: Haunting and the Sociological Imagination* (Minneapolis: University of Minnesota Press, 1997), 8.

11. Lisa Marie Cacho, *Social Death: Racialized Rightlessness and the Criminalization of the Unprotected* (New York: NYU Press, 2012), 99.

12. Robin DiAngelo, *White Fragility: Why It's So Hard for White People to Talk about Racism* (Boston: Beacon Press, 2018).

13. David Marriott, *Haunted Life: Visual Culture and Black Modernity* (New Brunswick, N.J.: Rutgers University Press, 2007), xxi.

14. In his work on visuality and surveillance, Nicholas Mirzoeff contends that "the deployment of visuality and visual technologies as a Western social technique for ordering was decisively shaped by the experience of plantation slavery in the Americas." For him, "modern" ways of seeing are inextricably bound up with slavery. See *The Right to Look: A Counterhistory of Visuality* (Durham, N.C.: Duke University Press, 2011), 48.

15. Alexander Weheliye, *Habeas Viscus: Racializing Assemblages, Biopolitics, and Black Feminist Theories of the Human* (Durham, N.C.: Duke University Press, 2014), 110.

16. See Hortense Spillers, "Mama's Baby, Papa's Maybe: An American Grammar Book," *Diacritics* 17, no. 2 (1987): 64–81; Jennifer Morgan, *Laboring Women: Reproduction and Gender in New World Slavery* (Philadelphia: University of Pennsylvania Press, 2004); and Brown, *Repeating Body*.

17. Ask a Slave: The Web Series, "Ask a Slave Ep 5: Two Sides to Every Coin," September 22, 2013, YouTube video, 2:41, https://www.youtube.com/watch?v=pYQbrdXIK04.

18. Ask a Slave: The Web Series, "Ask a Slave S2 Ep1: True Story," November 11, 2013, YouTube video, 3:25, https://www.youtube.com/watch?v=qD4U-4HT2xI.

19. See Howard Winant, *The World Is a Ghetto: Race and Democracy Since World War II* (New York: Basic Books, 2001); Jodi Melamed, *Represent and Destroy: Rationalizing Violence in the New Racial Capitalism* (Minneapolis: University of Minnesota Press, 2011); and Roderick Ferguson, *The Reorder of Things: The University and Its Pedagogies of Minority Difference* (Minneapolis: University of Minnesota Press, 2012).

20. Melamed, *Represent and Destroy*, 6.

21. See Winant, *World Is a Ghetto*; Melamed, *Represent and Destroy*;

Anna McCarthy, *The Citizen Machine: Governing by Television in 1950s America* (New York: New Press, 2010); and Ferguson, *Reorder of Things*.

22. For histories and analysis of neoliberalism, see David Harvey, *A Brief History of Neoliberalism* (New York: Oxford University Press, 2005); Lisa Duggan, *The Twilight of Equality? Neoliberalism, Cultural Politics, and the Attack on Democracy* (Boston: Beacon Press, 2004); and Julie Wilson, *Neoliberalism* (New York: Routledge, 2018).

23. Steve Martinot, *The Machinery of Whiteness: Studies in the Structure of Racialization* (Philadelphia: Temple University Press, 2010), 69. See also Matthew Frye Jacobson, *Whiteness of a Different Color: European Immigrants and the Alchemy of Race* (Cambridge, Mass.: Harvard University Press, 1999).

24. Walter Johnson, *Soul by Soul: Life inside the Antebellum Slave Market* (Cambridge, Mass.: Harvard University Press, 1999), 81–101.

25. Kyla Schuller, *The Biopolitics of Feeling: Race, Sex, and Science in the Nineteenth Century* (Durham, N.C.: Duke University Press, 2017), 2.

26. Michel Foucault, "Governmentality," in *The Foucault Effect: Studies in Governmentality*, ed. Graham Burchell et al. (Chicago: University of Chicago Press, 1991), 103.

27. Laurie Ouellette and James Hay, *Better Living through Reality TV* (Malden, Mass.: Blackwell, 2008), 8–18.

28. McCarthy, *Citizen Machine*.

29. For approaches to media and governmentality, see Ouellette and Hay, *Better Living through Reality TV*; Jodi Dean, *Democracy and Other Neoliberal Fantasies: Communicative Capitalism and Left Politics* (Durham, N.C.: Duke University Press, 2009); Jack Bratich, Jeremy Packer, and Cameron McCarthy, eds., *Foucault, Cultural Studies, and Governmentality* (Albany: State University of New York Press, 2003); and Lee Grieveson, *Policing Cinema: Movies and Censorship in Early Twentieth-Century America* (Berkeley: University of California Press, 2004).

30. Herman Gray, "Subject(ed) to Recognition," *American Quarterly* 65, no. 4 (2013): 777.

31. Gray, "Subject(ed) to Recognition," 772.

32. See Bratich, Packer, and McCarthy, *Foucault, Cultural Studies, and Governmentality*.

33. Ouellette and Hay, *Better Living through Reality TV*, 12.

34. Majia Nadesan, *Governing Childhood into the 21st Century: Biopolitical Technologies of Childhood Management and Education* (New York: Palgrave Macmillan, 2010), 8.

35. Philip Nobile and Maureen Kenney, "Congress Passed an Ethnic

Heritage Studies Program Act in 1974 to Encourage Looking Backward," *New York Times*, February 27, 1977, 150.

36. Sasha Torres, *Black, White, and in Color: Television and Black Civil Rights* (Princeton, N.J.: Princeton University Press, 2003), 6.

37. Carole Stabile, *White Victims, Black Villains: Gender, Race, and Crime News in US Culture* (New York: Routledge, 2006), 136. See also Fred MacDonald, *Blacks and White TV: Afro-Americans in Television since 1948* (Chicago: Nelson-Hall, 1983). The quiz show scandals undercut television's legitimacy at the moment of its increasing ubiquity and popularity.

38. Stanton quoted in MacDonald, *Blacks and White TV*, 107.

39. "Immerse Your Students in U.S. History with Mission US," Iowa PBS, June 8, 2021, https://www.iowapbs.org/education/story/27927/immerse-your-students-us-history-mission-us.

40. See, for example, Toni Morrison, *Song of Solomon* (New York: Knopf, 1977); Toni Morrison, *The Bluest Eye* (New York: Holt, Rinehart and Winston, 1970); Toni Cade Bambara, *The Sea Birds Are Still Alive: Collected Stories* (New York: Random House, 1977); Toni Cade Bambara, *The Salt Eaters* (New York: Random House, 1980); and Margaret Walker, *Jubilee* (New York: Bantam Books, 1966).

41. Ask a Slave: The Web Series, "Ask a Slave Ep 4: New Leaf, Same Page," September 15, 2013, YouTube video, 4:09, https://www.youtube.com/watch?v=ik-fXNjxw58.

1. "The Restless Black Peril"

1. Wolff quoted in Robert Musel, "'Heritage of Slavery' Next in CBS Series," *Los Angeles Times*, August 10, 1968, B3.

2. For more on how whiteness is produced through Blackness, see Walter Johnson, *Soul by Soul: Life inside the Antebellum Slave Market* (Cambridge, Mass.: Harvard University Press, 1999); Saidiya Hartman, *Scenes of Subjection: Terror, Slavery, and Self-Making in Nineteenth-Century America* (New York: Oxford University Press, 1997); David Roediger, *Wages of Whiteness: Race and the Making of the American Working Class* (New York: Verso, 2007); Cheryl Harris, "Whiteness as Property," *Harvard Law Review* 106, no. 8 (1993): 1710–45; Matthew Frye Jacobson, *Whiteness of a Different Color: European Immigrants and the Alchemy of Race* (Cambridge, Mass.: Harvard University Press, 1999); and Stephanie Smallwood, *Salt-water Slavery: A Middle Passage from Africa to America* (Cambridge, Mass.: Harvard University Press, 2007).

3. Michael Curtin, *Redeeming the Wasteland: Television Documentary*

and Cold War Politics (New Brunswick, N.J.: Rutgers University Press, 1995), 175.

4. See, for example, Kyla Schuller, *The Biopolitics of Feeling: Race, Sex, and Science in the Nineteenth Century* (Durham, N.C.: Duke University Press, 2018).

5. Bill Nichols, *Representing Reality: Issues and Concepts in Documentary* (Bloomington: Indiana University Press, 1991), 3.

6. Glenda Carpio, *Laughing Fit to Kill: Black Humor in the Fictions of Slavery* (New York: Oxford University Press, 2008), 18.

7. On May 9, 1961, Chair of the Federal Communications Commission Newton Minow famously referred to television as a "vast wasteland" during his "Television and the Public Interest" speech addressed to the National Association of Broadcasters. Available at http://www.american rhetoric.com/speeches/newtonminow.htm.

8. A. William Bluem, *Documentary in American Television: Form, Function, Method* (New York: Hastings House, 1965), 130–31.

9. See Curtin, *Redeeming the Wasteland.*

10. Nancy Fraser and Linda Gordon, "A Genealogy of Dependency: Tracing a Keyword of the U.S. Welfare State," *Signs* 19, no. 2 (1994): 328.

11. Daniel P. Moynihan, *The Negro Family: The Case for National Action* (Washington, D.C.: Office of Policy Planning and Research, United States Department of Labor, 1965), 15–17.

12. Daryl Michael Scott, *Contempt and Pity: Social Policy and the Image of the Damaged Black Psyche, 1880–1996* (Chapel Hill: University of North Carolina Press, 1997), 94.

13. Scott, *Contempt and Pity,* 154.

14. Scott, *Contempt and Pity,* xiii.

15. See, for example, Nikhil Singh, *Black Is a Country: Race and the Unfinished Struggle for Democracy* (Cambridge, Mass.: Harvard University Press, 2004); Howard Winant, *The World Is a Ghetto: Race and Democracy Since World War II* (New York: Basic Books, 2001); Mae Ngai, *Impossible Subjects: Illegal Aliens and the Making of Modern America* (Princeton, N.J.: Princeton University Press, 2004); and Jacobson, *Whiteness of a Different Color.*

16. Jodi Melamed, *Represent and Destroy: Rationalizing Violence in the New Racial Capitalism* (Minneapolis: University of Minnesota Press, 2011), ix.

17. Melamed, *Represent and Destroy,* x.

18. Roderick Ferguson, *The Reorder of Things: The University and Its Pedagogies of Minority Difference* (Minneapolis: University of Minnesota Press, 2012), 58.

19. Steve Martinot, *The Machinery of Whiteness: Studies in the Structure of Racialization* (Philadelphia: Temple University Press, 2010), 70.

20. Martinot, *Machinery of Whiteness*, 69.

21. Women are completely occluded in this discourse, which is significant given that cultural attention in later decades would shift to the racialized figure of the "angry Black woman." Thank you to Diane Negra for drawing my attention to this connection.

22. Brian Winston, *Claiming the Real II: Documentary; Grierson and Beyond* (New York: Palgrave Macmillan, 2008), 14.

23. Winston, *Claiming the Real II*, 7, 9.

24. Curtin, *Redeeming the Wasteland*, 15–16.

25. Curtin, *Redeeming the Wasteland*, 9. This quotation erases Black women by separating "women" and "African Americans."

26. Bluem, *Documentary in American Television*, 110–11.

27. Gareth Palmer, *Discipline and Liberty: Television and Governance* (Manchester, U.K.: Manchester University Press, 2003), 7.

28. 87 Cong. Rec. 107 (January 20, 1961) (Senator William Proxmire, speaking on "Cast the First Stone").

29. 87 Cong. Rec. 107 (January 20, 1961) (Senator William Proxmire, speaking on "Cast the First Stone").

30. Anna McCarthy, *The Citizen Machine: Governing by Television in 1950s America* (New York: New Press, 2010), 8.

31. John Daly, commentator, in *Bell & Howell Close-Up!*, episode 1, "Cast the First Stone," directed by Marshal Diskin, first aired September 27, 1960, on ABC. Viewed at the Paley Center for Media, New York.

32. Daly, "Cast the First Stone."

33. In his germinal essay on inferential versus structural racism, Stuart Hall examines television documentary to contend that media both consciously and unconsciously "define and construct the question of race in such a way as to reproduce the ideologies of racism." Stuart Hall, "The Whites of Their Eyes: Racist Ideologies and the Media," in *Silver Linings: Some Strategies for the Eighties*, ed. George Bridges and Rosalind Brunt, 28–52 (London: Lawrence and Wishart, 1981), 28.

34. Daly, "Cast the First Stone."

35. On the decoupling of race and whiteness, wherein the latter was translated into ethnicity, see Ngai, *Impossible Subjects*; and Jacobson, *Whiteness of a Different Color*.

36. Jacobson, *Whiteness of a Different Color*, 246.

37. Matthew Frye Jacobson, *Roots Too: White Ethnic Revival in Post–Civil Rights America* (Cambridge, Mass.: Harvard University Press, 2006), 33.

38. Daly, "Cast the First Stone."

39. Daly, "Cast the First Stone."

40. Daly, "Cast the First Stone." It is worth noting that the field of intercultural communication emerged during this same time period.

41. Daly, "Cast the First Stone."

42. Daly, "Cast the First Stone."

43. Ferguson, *Reorder of Things*, 58.

44. George Foster, reporter, in *Of Black America*, episode 5, "The Heritage of Slavery," produced by Perry Wolff, first aired August 13, 1968, on CBS. Viewed at the Paley Center for Media, New York.

45. Wolff quoted in Geoff Alexander, *Academic Films for the Classroom: A History* (Jefferson, N.C.: McFarland, 2010), 129.

46. *Bell & Howell Close-Up!*, episode 14, "Walk in My Shoes," directed by Nicholas Webster, first aired September 19, 1961, on ABC. Viewed at the Paley Center for Media, New York.

47. Curtin, *Redeeming the Wasteland*, 174.

48. Daly, "Cast the First Stone."

49. See Jonathan Metzl, *The Protest Psychosis: How Schizophrenia Became a Black Disease* (Boston: Beacon, 2009).

50. Amber Jamilla Musser, *Sensational Flesh: Race, Power, and Masochism* (New York: NYU Press, 2014), 117.

51. Scott, *Contempt and Pity*, 98.

52. This book provided just one of many so-called explanations for Black anger during this era. As Jonathan Metzl emphasizes, a 1964 *New York Times* article reviewed a "series of books that analyzed the increasingly 'violent and irrational' language of the civil rights movement, and particularly Black power, which often caused the 'average American' to feel 'worried and bewildered.'" See Metzl, *Protest Psychosis*, 113.

53. Scott, *Contempt and Pity*, 102–3.

54. Scott, *Contempt and Pity*, 110, 111, citing C. Eric Lincoln, *The Black Muslims in America* (Boston: Beacon Press, 1973).

55. Metzl, *Protest Psychosis*, xiv.

56. Metzl, *Protest Psychosis*, 103.

57. Harry Reasoner, reporter, *CBS Reports*, episode "The Harlem Temper," produced by Fred Friendly, first aired December 11, 1963, on CBS. Viewed at the Paley Center for Media, New York.

58. Saidiya Hartman, *Lose Your Mother: A Journey along the Atlantic Slave Route* (New York: Farrar, Straus and Giroux, 2007), 6.

59. Hartman, *Lose Your Mother*, 6.

60. Reasoner, "Harlem Temper."

61. Reasoner, "Harlem Temper."

62. Scott, *Contempt and Pity*, 113–14.

63. In his work on 1960s and 1970s New Left activism and media, Todd Gitlin argues that news media treated antiwar activism as unruly, threatening, and pathological. See Gitlin, *The Whole World Is Watching: Mass Media and the Making and Unmaking of the New Left* (Berkeley: University of California Press, 2003). Similarly, Susan Douglas shows how news coverage of feminist action during the 1970s described feminism as a "contagion," thereby likening it to a social disease. See Douglas, *Where the Girls Are: Growing Up Female with the Mass Media* (New York: Three Rivers, 1995), 164–91.

64. This (white) anxiety reemerged during Barack Obama's election, when some white people—led by the Tea Party—feared that a Black president would make white citizens "pay" for slavery. Tea Party rallies featured signs stating "Obama Plans White Slavery." See Ta-Nehisi Coates, "Fear of a Black President," *Atlantic*, September 2012, http://www.theatlantic.com/magazine/archive/2012/09/fear-of-a-black-president/309064/.

65. Foster, "Heritage of Slavery."

66. In *Roots Too*, Matthew Frye Jacobson describes the shift from a national discourse about origins in Plymouth, Massachusetts, to a nation of immigrants in the 1960s. Jacobson, "Hyphen Nation," in *Roots Too*, 11–71.

67. For a theorization of how slavery "possesses" the present, see Stephen Dillon, "Possessed by Death: The Neoliberal-Carceral State, Black Feminism, and the Afterlife of Slavery," *Radical History Review* 112 (2012): 113–25.

68. Carole Stabile, *White Victims, Black Villains: Gender, Race, and Crime News in U.S. Culture* (New York: Routledge, 2006), 152. The equation of Blackness with criminality has a long history rooted in slavery. See, for example, Nikhil Pal Singh, "The Whiteness of Police," *American Quarterly* 66, no. 4 (2014): 1091–99.

69. Mike Wallace, reporter, *CBS Reports*, episode "Black Power, White Backlash," produced by Alice Bigart and Sam Roberts, directed by Joe Gorsuch, first aired September 27, 1966, on CBS.

70. Wallace, "Black Power, White Backlash."

71. Stephen Best and Saidiya Hartman, "Fugitive Justice," *Representations* 92 (2005): 9. It is worth noting that Carmichael was staunchly critical of capitalism.

72. Wallace, "Black Power, White Backlash."

73. Wallace, "Black Power, White Backlash."

74. Harris in Wallace, "Black Power, White Backlash."

75. Harris in Wallace, "Black Power, White Backlash."

76. Aniko Bodroghkozy, *Equal Time: Television and the Civil Rights Movement* (Urbana: University of Illinois Press, 2012), 3.

77. Wallace, "Black Power, White Backlash."

78. As J. Fred MacDonald notes, "Commercial TV rediscovered African-American problems in 1968." According to MacDonald, during the summer of 1968, network television aired twenty documentaries focusing on "Black problems," including the seven-part CBS series *Of Black America*. MacDonald, *Blacks and White TV: Afro-Americans in Television since 1948* (Chicago: Nelson-Hall, 1983), 145–47.

79. MacDonald, *Blacks and White TV*, 146.

80. This discourse is also rooted in class and gender—the ideal citizen is a middle-class white man.

81. Robert Wright, "Advertising: Accolades for 'Black America,'" *New York Times*, August 29, 1968, 57.

82. George Gent, "Show on Negroes Arouses Viewers," *New York Times*, July 4, 1968, 41.

83. Ed Dowling, "Color Us Black," *New Republic*, June 8, 1968.

84. Doris Innis, "TV Review: A Flawed Breakthrough on Blackness," *Life*, August 9, 1968. In the August 30, 1968, issue of *Life*, a white letter writer thanked Doris Innis for her review: "I was so glad to read Doris Innis' review of *Of Black America*. More commentaries by blacks on specific events are certainly helping to sensitive [*sic*] us whites to the unintended wounds we are inflicting. Dorothy Bawden, Laguna Hills, Calif." *Life*, August 30, 1968.

85. Foster, "Heritage of Slavery."

86. Musser, *Sensational Flesh*, 101–2.

2. Feeling Slavery

1. Jordan quoted in William Marmon, "Why 'Roots' Hit Home," *Time*, February 14, 1977.

2. Jennifer Petersen, "Media as Sentimental Education: The Political Lessons of HBO's *The Laramie Project* and PBS's *Two Towns of Jasper*," *Critical Studies in Media Communication* 26, no. 3 (2009): 258.

3. Roderick Ferguson, *The Reorder of Things: The University and Its Pedagogies of Minority Difference* (Minneapolis: University of Minnesota Press, 2012).

4. Miami-Dade Community College, "Roots: Offering 'Roots' for College and University Level Study," brochure, box 304, file 7330, David L. Wolper Collection, University of Southern California, Los Angeles.

5. Miami-Dade Community College, Office of Information Services,

"Roots of Black Americans: A Unique History," brochure, box 304, file 7330, David L. Wolper Collection, University of Southern California, Los Angeles.

6. Matthew Frye Jacobson, *Roots Too: White Ethnic Revival in Post–Civil Rights America* (Cambridge, Mass.: Harvard University Press, 2006), 54.

7. Jacobson, *Roots Too*, 54–55.

8. Glenda Carpio, *Laughing Fit to Kill: Black Humor in the Fictions of Slavery* (New York: Oxford University Press, 2008), 12.

9. Miami-Dade Community College, "Roots: Offering 'Roots' for College and University Level Study."

10. It is significant that *Gone with the Wind* was a deeply romanticized and nostalgic portrayal of slavery and white supremacy. See Linda Williams, *Playing the Race Card: Melodramas of Black and White from Uncle Tom to O.J. Simpson* (Princeton, N.J.: Princeton University Press, 2001), 238–39.

11. ABC Press Relations, "Cities and Colleges Honor 'Roots,'" Press Release, January 19, 1977, box 283, file 6930, David L. Wolper Collection, University of Southern California, Los Angeles; and Arlene Wolff to Tina Legg, January 18, 1977, box 283, file 6956, David L. Wolper Collection, University of Southern California, Los Angeles.

12. As the "'sole non-theatrical film distributor of *Roots*,' Films Incorporated also produced *Roots*-related audiotapes, StoryStrip and MovieStrip activities, lesson plans, and teacher's guides." Films Incorporated, "Roots: A best seller . . . the television event of 1977 . . . and a celebrated movie from Films Incorporated," promotional packet for educators, box 304, file 7335, David L. Wolper Collection, University of Southern California, Los Angeles. See also Geoff Alexander, *Academic Films for the Classroom: A History* (Jefferson, N.C.: McFarland, 2010), 100–1.

13. David L. Wolper and Quincy Troupe, *The Inside Story of T.V.'s "Roots"* (New York: Warner, 1978), 23.

14. Wolper was a key figure advocating for a combination of education with entertainment—"edutainment"—in media. See Wolper and Troupe, *Inside Story of T.V.'s "Roots."*

15. Robert Sklar, interview notes with David Wolper, p. 4, box 304, file 7345, David L. Wolper Collection, University of Southern California, Los Angeles.

16. Julie Passanante Elman, *Chronic Youth: Disability, Sexuality, and U.S. Media Cultures of Rehabilitation* (New York: NYU Press, 2014), 4.

17. Frank Wells to David Wolper, April 26, 1977, box 304, file 7321, David L. Wolper Collection, University of Southern California, Los Angeles. Educators were similarly involved in *Roots: The Next Generations*. Ac-

cording to a 1979 PR letter, the National Education Association's research department estimated that "a half million NEA Social Studies teachers assigned their students to watch 'Roots: The Next Generations.' Because many of these teachers instruct 4–5 separate classes, the NEA estimates that close to 20 million students viewed the program as part of a classroom assignment." Pamela Warford to Those listed below, March 21, 1979, box 304, file 7321, David L. Wolper Collection, University of Southern California, Los Angeles. See also William Van Deburg, *Slavery and Race in American Popular Culture* (Madison: University of Wisconsin Press, 1984), 155.

18. Linley Stafford to David L. Wolper, box 304, file 7321, David L. Wolper Collection, University of Southern California, Los Angeles.

19. Patricia Clough, *The User Unconscious: On Affect, Media, and Measure* (Minneapolis: University of Minnesota Press, 2018), 121–22.

20. Films Incorporated, Teacher's Guide Grades 7-College, box 304, file 7328, David L. Wolper Collection, University of Southern California, Los Angeles.

21. Gayle Wald, *It's Been Beautiful: "Soul!" and Black Power Television* (Durham, N.C.: Duke University Press, 2015), 21.

22. Wald, *It's Been Beautiful*, 30.

23. Nikhil Singh, *Black Is a Country: Race and the Unfinished Struggle for Democracy* (Cambridge, Mass.: Harvard University Press, 2005), 181, 193.

24. Singh, *Black Is a Country*, 188.

25. Singh, 191.

26. Sally Reed, "Alex Haley's Tips for 'Roots' Projects," *Instructor*, October 1977, 93–94.

27. Miami-Dade Community College, "Roots: Offering 'Roots' for College and University Level Study," "The Experience of Ellen Heidt," Language Arts Instructor, teaching a 'Roots' course," brochure, box 304, file 7330, David L. Wolper Collection, University of Southern California, Los Angeles.

28. Willard McGuire, "An Interview with Alex Haley," *Today's Education*, September/October 1977, http://www.alex-haley.com/alex_haley_willard_mcguire_interview.htm.

29. Elman, *Chronic Youth*, 96.

30. Miami-Dade Community College, "Roots of Black Americans."

31. Margaret H. Campbell, "Africa, Roots, and Pride for Afro-Americans: An Instructional Unit," teacher's guide, Illinois University, Urbana, African Studies Program, July 1977, http://eric.ed.gov/?id=ED189007.

32. Jonathan Metzl, *The Protest Psychosis: How Schizophrenia Became a Black Disease* (Boston: Beacon, 2009), 114.

33. Van Deburg, *Slavery and Race in American Popular Culture*, 155.

34. "The Soul Market in Black and White," *Sales Management* 102 (June 1, 1969): 31–41, quoted in Robert Weems Jr., *Desegregating the Dollar: African American Consumerism in the Twentieth Century* (New York: New York University Press, 1998), 76–77.

35. Jacobson, *Roots Too*, 2.

36. Jacobson, 21.

37. Jacobson, 54.

38. Reed, "Alex Haley's Tips for 'Roots' Projects," 96.

39. In the curriculum on Black pride developed by Margaret Campbell, she includes "Africa has no history" on a list of ten "Common Stereotypes about Africa which are NOT accurate." Teachers are instructed to have students correct these statements based on information taught in class. Campbell, "Africa, Roots, and Pride for Afro-Americans."

40. Saidiya Hartman, *Lose Your Mother: A Journey along the Atlantic Slave Route* (New York: Farrar, Straus and Giroux, 2007), 100.

41. Ferguson, *Reorder of Things*, 84.

42. Michael Kirkhorn, "A Saga of Slavery That Made the Actors Weep," *New York Times*, June 27, 1976, 47.

43. Alex Haley to Stan Margulies, September 20, 1975, box 105, file 001, David L. Wolper Collection, University of Southern California, Los Angeles.

44. See Sarah Banet-Weiser, "What's Your Flava? Race and Postfeminism in Media Culture," in *Interrogating Postfeminism: Gender and the Politics of Popular Culture*, ed. Yvonne Tasker and Diane Negra, 201–25 (Durham, N.C.: Duke University Press, 2007).

45. "Haley Criticizes Bicentennial Protest," *Daily Nebraskan*, February 8, 1976, box 106, file 009, David L. Wolper Collection, University of Southern California, Los Angeles. It is worth noting that one such critique came from Richard Pryor on his 1976 album *Bicentennial Nigger*, which critiques the celebratory narrative of the Bicentennial. As Glenda Carpio notes, by "declaring his commitment 'never to forget' his country's history of genocide and enslavement precisely when bicentennial celebrations would obfuscate it, Pryor not only performs the previously segregated aspects of black humor—its aggressive, political, and nuanced aspects—but also roots the birth of that humor in slavery." *Laughing Fit to Kill*, 77.

46. Films Incorporated, "Teacher's Guide to Roots for Elementary Grades," box 304, file 7328, David L. Wolper Collection, University of Southern California, Los Angeles. The title of this unit refers to the final scene of *Roots* before Alex Haley appears, where Kunta Kinte's ancestor George describes the legacy of freedom passed down to him: "Before he

die, he give that dream of freedom to his daughter; Kizzy, my mama. And before she die, she give that dream to me, and I've tried to keep that dream alive in all you children till that day come. Hear me, O African. The flesh of your flesh has come to freedom. You is free at last. We is free." *Roots*, directed by David Greene and John Erman (1977; Burbank, Calif.: Warner Home Video, 2011), DVD.

47. Films Incorporated, "Teacher's Guide to Roots for Elementary Grades."

48. Rebecca Wanzo, *The Suffering Will Not Be Televised: African American Women and Sentimental Political Storytelling* (Albany: SUNY Press, 2009), 39.

49. Films Incorporated, "Teacher's Guide to Roots for Elementary Grades."

50. Wanzo, *Suffering Will Not Be Televised*, 40.

51. Saidiya Hartman, *Scenes of Subjection: Terror, Slavery, and Self-Making in Nineteenth-Century America* (New York: Oxford University Press, 1997), 20.

52. Alexander Weheliye, *Habeus Viscus: Racializing Assemblages, Biopolitics, and Black Feminist Theories of the Human* (Durham, N.C.: Duke University Press, 2014), 14.

53. Films Incorporated, "Teacher's Guide to Roots for Elementary Grades."

54. Films Incorporated (emphasis added).

55. Angela Davis, "Reflections on the Black Woman's Role in the Community of Slaves," in *The Angela Y. Davis Reader*, ed. Joy James (Malden, Mass.: Blackwell, 1998), 125.

56. Davis, "Reflections on the Black Woman's Role in the Community of Slaves," 117.

57. Davis, 123.

58. Davis, 118.

59. Davis, 123.

60. Maryemma Graham, *Conversations with Margaret Walker* (Jackson: University Press of Mississippi, 2002), 133.

61. Margaret Wilkerson, introduction to *Les Blancs: The Collected Last Plays: The Drinking Gourd/What Use Are Flowers?*, ed. Robert Nemiroff (New York: Vintage Books, 1994), 14.

62. Imani Perry, *Looking for Lorraine: The Radiant and Radical Life of Lorraine Hansberry* (Boston: Beacon, 2018), 159.

63. Robert Nemiroff to Grant A. Tinker, Chairman of the Board of NBC, April 5, 1982, box 43, folder 10, Schomburg Center for Research in Black Culture, New York.

64. Robert Nemiroff, ed., *Les Blancs: The Collected Last Plays: The Drinking Gourd/What Use Are Flowers* (New York: Vintage Books, 1994), 152.

65. Nemiroff, *Les Blancs,* 153.

66. Wilkerson, introduction, 14.

67. Lorraine Hansberry, *The Drinking Gourd,* in Nemiroff, *Les Blancs,* 167.

68. Perry, *Looking for Lorraine,* 159.

69. Hansberry, *Drinking Gourd,* 196.

70. Hansberry, 188.

71. Erica Ball and Kellie Carter Jackson, introduction to *Reconsidering Roots: Race, Politics, and Memory* (Athens: University of Georgia Press, 2017), 7.

72. Hansberry, *Drinking Gourd,* 153.

73. Hansberry, 184.

74. Cheryl Harris, "Whiteness as Property," in *Critical Race Theory: The Key Writings That Formed the Movement,* ed. Kimberlé Crenshaw et al., 276–90 (New York: New Press, 1995).

75. Wanzo, *Suffering Will Not Be Televised,* 39.

76. Williams, *Playing the Race Card,* xiv.

77. Williams, 299.

78. Williams, xv.

79. Jennifer Petersen, *Murder, the Media, and the Politics of Public Feelings: Remembering Matthew Shepard and James Byrd Jr.* (Bloomington: Indiana University Press, 2011), 97.

80. Hartman, *Scenes of Subjection,* 25–28.

81. Ahmed, *Cultural Politics of Emotion,* 21.

82. Lisa Cacho traces how the deployment of difference renders particular populations vulnerable to premature or social death by marking them as worthless and valueless under white supremacist and capitalist logics. See *Social Death: Racialized Rightlessness and the Criminalization of the Unprotected* (New York: NYU Press, 2012).

83. Robert H. McCabe to Colleges and Universities Interested in the "Roots" Course, box 304, file 7330, David L. Wolper Collection, University of Southern California, Los Angeles. Emphasis added.

84. Miami-Dade Community College, "Administrative Guide for a Unique History Course Based on <u>ROOTS</u>," October 1976, p. 2, "Recruitment," box 304, file 7331, David L. Wolper Collection, University of Southern California, Los Angeles.

85. Films Incorporated, "Teacher's Guide to Roots for Elementary Grades."

86. Miami-Dade Community College, "What Do Students Say about

the Television Series on Roots?" packet, box 304, file 7335, David L. Wolper Collection, University of Southern California, Los Angeles.

87. Miami-Dade Community College, "What Do Students Say about the Television Series on Roots?"

88. Wanzo, *Suffering Will Not Be Televised*, 3.

89. Jacobson, *Roots Too*, 43.

90. Barbara Cruikshank, *The Will to Empower: Democratic Citizens and Other Subjects* (Ithaca, N.Y.: Cornell University Press, 1999), 80, 105, 111. The logic of empowerment as a response to poverty has only grown in recent decades as neoliberalism has become further entrenched.

91. George Lipsitz, *The Possessive Investment in Whiteness: How White People Profit from Identity Politics* (Philadelphia: Temple University Press, 1998), 7.

92. David Freund, *Colored Property: State Policy and White Racial Politics in Suburban America* (Chicago: University of Chicago Press, 2007), 383–85.

93. Freund, *Colored Property*, 384.

94. Lipsitz, *Possessive Investment in Whiteness*, 6.

95. Douglas Massey and Nancy Denton, *American Apartheid: Segregation and the Making of the Underclass* (Cambridge, Mass.: Harvard University Press, 1993), 49.

96. Massey and Denton, *American Apartheid*, 61.

97. Lipsitz, *Possessive Investment in Whiteness*, 18.

98. See Harris, "Whiteness as Property."

99. Melvin Oliver and Thomas Shapiro, *Black Wealth/White Wealth: A New Perspective on Racial Inequality* (New York: Routledge, 2006), 24.

100. Oliver and Shapiro, *Black Wealth/White Wealth*, 94.

101. Lipsitz, *Possessive Investment in Whiteness*, 3.

102. According to historian Jessica Johnson, there was an attempt during the early 1970s to move the history of slavery into the realm of numerals and statistics as a way to drain emotion from historical scholarship. Turning to data was a supposedly neutral and emotionally detached way to examine the history of slavery. This is perhaps most evident in the economists Robert William Fogel and Stanley L. Engerman's controversial book from 1974, *Time on the Cross: The Economics of American Negro Slavery*, which described the everyday lives of slaves through data, coming to the conclusion that material lives for Black people were "better" under slavery. Jessica Johnson, "Death Acts, Haunting, and Other Curious Adventures" (presentation, Amherst College, Amherst, Mass., March 29, 2016).

103. Lauren Tucker and Hermant Shah, "Race and the Transformation

of Culture: The Making of the Television Miniseries *Roots,*" *Critical Studies in Mass Communication* 9 (1992): 328.

104. David L. Wolper to Brandon Stoddard, August 17, 1978, box 282, file 6918, David L. Wolper Collection, University of Southern California, Los Angeles.

105. Tucker and Shah, "Race and the Transformation of Culture," 328–29.

106. Wolper and Troupe, *Inside Story of T.V.'s "Roots,"* 18.

107. Stan Margulies to David L. Wolper et al., June 7, 1976, box 106, file 009, David L. Wolper Collection, University of Southern California, Los Angeles.

108. "Suggested Viewer Advisory," October 6, 1976, box 282, file 6908, David L. Wolper Collection, University of Southern California, Los Angeles.

109. ABC Department of Broadcast Standards and Practices, report, March 16, 1976, box 104, file 024, David L. Wolper Collection, University of Southern California, Los Angeles.

110. ABC Department of Broadcast Standards and Practices, report, March 16, 1976, box 104, file 024, David L. Wolper Collection, University of Southern California, Los Angeles. Emphasis added.

111. American Broadcasting Company, Department of Broadcast Standards and Practices, Western Division, Ronald W. Taylor, Editor, box 104, file 024, March 16, 1976, David L. Wolper Collection, University of Southern California, Los Angeles.

112. Patricia Hill Collins, *Black Sexual Politics: African Americans, Gender, and the New Racism* (New York: Routledge, 2004), 219.

113. Angela Davis, *Women, Race, and Class* (New York: Random House, 1981), 7.

114. American Broadcasting Company, Department of Broadcast Standards and Practices, Western Division, Ronald W. Taylor, Editor, box 104, file 024, March 16, 1976, David L. Wolper Collection, University of Southern California, Los Angeles.

115. American Broadcasting Company, Department of Broadcast Standards and Practices, Western Division, Ronald W. Taylor, Editor, box 104, file 024, March 16, 1976, David L. Wolper Collection, University of Southern California, Los Angeles.

116. Stan Margulies to Brandon Stoddard, May 11, 1976, box 104, file 024, David L. Wolper Collection, University of Southern California, Los Angeles.

117. Carol Stevens, Memo detailing ABC's first press release, June 14, 1976, box 106, file 009, David L. Wolper Collection, University of Southern California, Los Angeles.

118. Family Channel, Promotion, 1992, box 283, file 6934, David L. Wolper Collection, University of Southern California, Los Angeles. Emphasis added.

119. Miami-Dade Community College, "Roots of Black Americans."

120. For more on how white supremacy is adaptive, see Stephanie Smallwood, "Freedom," in *Keywords for American Cultural Studies*, 2nd ed., ed. Bruce Burgett and Glenn Hendler (New York: NYU Press, 2014).

121. Burton quoted in Bryn Sandberg, "Watch the First Trailer for History's 'Roots' Remake," *Hollywood Reporter*, February 11, 2016, https://www.hollywoodreporter.com/tv/tv-news/watch-first-trailer-historys-roots-864380/.

3. Choosing Freedom

1. The White House's Office of E-Government and Information Technology refers to educational games as "games for learning," whereas the industry uses "edugames."

2. Benjamin Herold, "Digital 'Slavery Simulation' Game for Schools Draws Ire, Praise," *Education Week*, February 17, 2015, http://blogs.edweek.org/edweek/DigitalEducation/2015/02/slavery_simulation_digital_game.html.

3. "What Is *Mission US*?" Mission US, http://www.mission-us.org/pages/about.

4. Billed as an "interactive way to learn history," *Mission US* is the joint product of a "multidisciplinary team" of scholars, educators, and game designers spearheaded by WNET and is freely available via the game's website. To date, there are six missions in total, including "A Cheyenne Odyssey," where users inhabit the character Little Fox, a "northern Cheyenne boy" in 1866; "City of Immigrants," featuring the character Lena Brodksy, a "14-year-old Jewish immigrant from Russia" emigrating to the United States in 1907; and "Prisoner in My Homeland," which asks, "When the government forces you [as 16-year-old Henry Tanaka] and 120,000 other innocent Japanese Americans into camps, how will you react?" "Play Mission US," Mission US, http://www.mission-us.org/play/.

5. "What Is *Mission US*?" Mission US.

6. Kellie Specter, "In Support of 'Flight to Freedom,' One of Many Ways to Teach History," *EdSurge*, February 18, 2015, https://www.edsurge.com/n/2015-02-18-in-support-of-flight-to-freedom-one-of-many-ways-to-teach-history. This piece is a response to Rafranz Davis's critique of *Flight to Freedom* by a member of WNET Education's team. It is important to note that the phrasing "enslaved African Americans" constitutes an oxymoron.

7. Walter Johnson, "On Agency," *Journal of Social History* 37 (2003): 117.

8. THIRTEEN/WNET New York, "Mission US: 'Flight to Freedom' Immerses Middle School Students in the History of Slavery and Abolition in a New Virtual Experience," Cision PR Newswire, January 24, 2012, https://www.prnewswire.com/news-releases/mission-us-flight-to -freedom-immerses-middle-school-students-in-the-history-of-slavery -and-abolition-in-a-new-virtual-experience-137973758.html.

9. Throughout this chapter, I draw on Walter Johnson's piece "On Agency" to theorize *Flight to Freedom*'s emphasis on agency. In the article, Johnson describes historians' attempts to bestow agency on slaves as a liberal maneuver, one that seeks to include slaves in a liberal narrative of history that emphasizes rationality, autonomy, individuality, and action. I use parentheses to highlight that for *Flight to Freedom,* this has implications for subject formation under advanced liberalism, thereby marking the forms of agency the game espouses as (neo)liberal.

10. Aubrey Anable, *Playing with Feelings: Video Games and Affect* (Minneapolis: University of Minnesota Press, 2018).

11. Mission US, "Mission 2: 'Flight to Freedom' Educator Guide," p. 272, http://www.mission-us.org/teach/flight-to-freedom/teaching -this-mission/about-m2/.

12. Specter, "In Support of 'Flight to Freedom.'"

13. Rafranz Davis, "Is a Slave Simulation Game Appropriate for Classrooms?" *EdSurge,* February 17, 2015, https://www.edsurge.com/n/2015 -02-17-opinion-slave-simulation-an-edtech-game-for-classrooms. Other critiques include the game's potential to traumatize students of color and the fact that the game does not hold white people or whiteness accountable in any way.

14. Herold, "Digital 'Slavery Simulation' Game."

15. "American History and Civics Initiative," Corporation for Public Broadcasting, http://www.cpb.org/grants/historyandcivics.

16. Laurie Ouellette, *Viewers Like You?: How Public TV Failed the People* (New York: Columbia University Press, 2002), 18, 21.

17. Ouellette, *Viewers Like You?,* 25.

18. Ouellette, *Viewers Like You?,* 72–73.

19. Chenm, "Mission US," Ideascale, February 13, 2014, 8:06 p.m., http://gamesforimpact.ideascale.com/a/dtd/Mission-US/26643-27305.

20. "About *Mission US,*" Mission US, https://www.mission-us.org/ about/.

21. "Projects: American History and Civics Initiative: Research on Digital Games and History Learning," Center for Children & Technology,

http://cct.edc.org/projects/american-history-and-civics-initiative
-research-digital-games-and-history-learning.

22. Ian Bogost, *Persuasive Games: The Expressive Power of Videogames* (Boston: MIT Press, 2007), 35.

23. Alexander Galloway, *Gaming: Essays on Algorithmic Culture* (Minneapolis: University of Minnesota Press, 2006), 71–72.

24. Peter Chow-White, "The Informationalization of Race: Communication Technologies and the Human Genome in the Digital Age," *International Journal of Communication* 2 (2008): 1171–72.

25. Chow-White, "Informationalization of Race," 1172.

26. Lisa Nakamura and Peter Chow-White, "Race and Digital Technology: Code, the Color Line, and the Information Society," in *Race After the Internet*, ed. Lisa Nakamura and Peter Chow-White (New York: Routledge, 2012), 8.

27. "Follow the North Star," Conner Prairie, accessed January 24, 2018, http://www.connerprairie.org/Things-To-Do/Events/Follow-the-North -Star. It is worth noting that at the end of the experience, participants are encouraged to combat slavery by downloading the Slavery Footprint app. In 2019, Connor Prairie announced that the Follow the North Star program would be "updated." "Good Morning: Conner Prairie to Change Its Follow the North Star Program," *Herald Bulletin,* April 22, 2019, https:// www.heraldbulletin.com/news/local_news/briefs/good-morning -conner-prairie-to-change-its-follow-the-north-star-program/ article_48ecefc8-47f2-50ea-b840-74f2e416fb1a.html.

28. This is the latest iteration in a long line of embodied attempts updated for the digital age and the notion of digital embodiment. See Lisa Woolfork, *Embodying American Slavery in Contemporary Culture* (Champaign: University of Illinois Press, 2008); and James Horton and Lois Horton, eds., *Slavery and Public History: The Tough Stuff of American Memory* (New York: New Press, 2006).

29. "Immerse Your Students in U.S. History with Mission US," Iowa PBS, October 1, 2017, https://www.iowapbs.org/education/story/27927/ immerse-your-students-us-history-mission-us.

30. MissionUS, "Mission US: 'Flight to Freedom' Overview," November 13, 2012, YouTube video, 5:50, https://www.youtube.com/watch?v= tIyu81mH-yI.

31. See Woolfork, *Embodying American Slavery in Contemporary Culture,* esp. "Ritual Reenactments" and "Historical Reenactments"; Salamishah Tillet, *Sites of Slavery: Citizenship and Racial Democracy in the Post–Civil Rights Imagination* (Durham, N.C.: Duke University Press, 2012); and Horton and Horton, *Slavery and Public History.*

32. "What Is *Mission US?*" Mission US.

33. MissionUS, "Mission US in the Classroom: 'Flight to Freedom' (Full Classroom Video)," November 13, 2012, YouTube video, 39:31, https://www.youtube.com/watch?v=939mEqm21EM.

34. Johnson, "On Agency," 119.

35. MissionUS, "Mission US in the Classroom," YouTube video.

36. Mission US, "Teacher's Guide: Content Briefing, Mission 2: 'Flight to Freedom,'" https://www.mission-us.org/teach/flight-to-freedom/teaching-this-mission/introduction/.

37. Paul C. Schuytema, "What Cost Freedom," *Compute!*, no. 156, September 1993, 82, http://www.atarimagazines.com/compute/issue156/82_What_cost_freedom.php.

38. "School's Computer Game on Slavery Prompts Suit," *New York Times*, August 28, 1995, http://www.nytimes.com/1995/08/28/us/school-s-computer-game-on-slavery-prompts-suit.html.

39. National Geographic, *The Underground Railroad*, http://media.nationalgeographic.org/assets/richmedia/0/195/project/j1.html; and Liz Dwyer, "Teachers and Gamers Agree: 'Slave Tetris' Isn't How You Educate Kids about Slavery," *Take Part*, September 1, 2015, http://www.takepart.com/article/2015/09/01/teachers-gamers-agree-slave-tetris-isnt-how-you-educate-kids-about-slavery.

40. See, for example, Debbe Thompson et al., "Serious Video Games for Health: How Behavioral Science Guided the Development of a Serious Video Game," *Simulation and Gaming* 41 (2010): 587–606. In this article, the authors explore a "serious" game designed to modify youth behavior around eating so as to address the rise of obesity and type-2 diabetes. Serious games are a particularly effective means of entertaining players "as they educate, train, or change behavior" in part because they embed "functional knowledge and change procedures" into an "immersive game environment (589). In line with demands to continuously improve and adapt oneself as a strategy for navigating precarity and an unstable job market, edutainment provides a way to make lifelong learning fun.

41. Other terms include "social impact" games, "games for change," and "socially conscious" games. Edugames, in particular, are part of what Aubrey Anable calls the "gamification" of everyday life, where arenas "once hostile to video games" like education, work, and public health now take up game play as a pedagogical or training tool. See Anable, "Casual Games, Time Management, and the Work of Affect," *Ada: A Journal of Gender, New Media, and Technology* 2 (2013): http://adanewmedia.org/2013/06/issue2-anable/. Jennifer deWinter, Carly A. Kocurek, and Randall Nichols critique the rise of gamification for its contribution to the ever-increasing

conflation of work and leisure, which they contend leads to a "values collapse" where the "values of the workplace and the values of play are the same." DeWinter, Kocurek, and Nichols, "Taylorism 2.0: Gamification, Scientific Management and the Capitalist Appropriation of Play," *Journal of Gaming and Virtual Worlds* 6, no. 2 (2014): 111. The potentially resistive possibilities of play are therefore eroded. When companies create corporate training games, the "algorithms of work" become entangled in the "algorithms of play," further normalizing the idea of "leisure time as something that should be productive" (111, 121). Contemporary gamification was anticipated during the 1950s with the creation of educational "business games." According to Rolf Nohr of the Digital Games Research Association, ex-military personnel, academics, and businesspeople began to create educational games after a "break of society's steering logic" in the postwar era. Crucially, such games reproduced "parts of specific economic, political or social systems" and provided a "simplified access to the complex correlations in these systems." See Rolf F. Nohr, "Business Games, Rationality, and Control Logistics," *DiGRA '11 Proceedings of the 2011 DiGRA International Conference: Think Design Play* 6 (2011): http://www.digra.org/digital-library/publications/business-games-rationality-and-control-logistics/. In a similar manner, *Flight to Freedom* reduces the history of U.S. chattel slavery to a series of individual decisions made by enslaved people, who are therefore made responsible for their freedom or lack thereof.

42. Bogost, *Persuasive Games*, 56–57.

43. David Nieborg, "Training Recruits and Conditioning Youth: The Soft Power of Military Games," in *Joystick Soldiers: The Politics of Play in Military Video Games*, ed. Nina Huntemann and Matthew Payne, 53–66 (New York: Routledge, 2010), 54.

44. Some game critics have called for games that enable players to actually change "core simulation dynamics to allow alternative perspectives"; *Mission US* does not allow players to change the rules of play. Bogost, *Persuasive Games*, 37.

45. Elizabeth Svoboda, "The Rise of the 'Gaming for Good' Movement," *Newsweek*, June 7, 2015, http://www.newsweek.com/rise-gaming-good-movement-340198.

46. "About Us," 3C Institute, https://www.3cisd.com/about.

47. "About Us," Games for Change, http://www.gamesforchange.org/who-we-are/about-us/. The impetus to combine gaming and education was supported by the Obama administration, which sought to foster pedagogical approaches that promised "interactive, personalized learning experiences driven by new technology." Brandon Griggs, "Obama Poised

to Be First 'Wired' President," CNN, January 15, 2009, http://www.cnn
.com/2009/TECH/01/15/obama.internet.president/. In March 2011, then
president Obama delivered a speech at TechBoston Academy in Boston,
Massachusetts, a college preparatory school for grades 6–12, "serving kids
from some of the toughest neighborhoods in Boston." After receiving
funding from Melinda Gates and the Gates Foundation, the school was
"turned . . . into one of [Boston's] most successful." TechBoston emphasizes a science, technology, engineering, and math (STEM) curriculum,
longer school days, and year-round schooling as solutions to the crises
of high school dropouts and lack of future job prospects for students
not equipped to enter STEM fields. During Obama's speech to students,
administrators, and policymakers, he highlighted TechBoston's "twenty-
first-century" focus and underscored the need for educational technology
to help students achieve skills for the new millennium. Such educational
technology, according to Obama, includes video games. In response to
his appeal for investments in enthralling educational software, more than
seventy government employees from agencies including the National Park
Service, the Army, and the National Endowment for the Arts convened
at the White House in November 2011 to "discuss games as a tool for addressing national problems," including education. Under the umbrella of
"games for change," the U.S. Department of Education and the Office of
Science and Technology Policy hosted an Ed Games Week in 2014 that
concluded with a forty-eight-hour White House Education Game Jam
where participants—"one hundred veteran and independent game developers, teachers, and students"—created playable prototypes of educational games. These games included "President of the Galaxy, a game about the
dynamics of U.S. presidential elections" and "NASA's Moonbase Alpha," a
game that had players "keep a base on the moon operational," which was
downloaded more than a million times. See Jesse Lee, "President Obama
Talks Education in Boston: 'A Moral and Economic Imperative to Give
Every Child the Chance to Succeed," White House (blog), March 8, 2011,
https://www.whitehouse.gov/blog/2011/03/08/president-obama-talks
-education-boston-moral-and-economic-imperative-give-every-chil; and
"Invite-Only Games for Learning Summit Set for Tuesday," Games and
Learning, April 19, 2015, https://www.gamesandlearning.org/2015/04/19/
invite-only-games-for-learning-summit-set-for-tuesday/.

48. Svoboda, "Rise of the 'Gaming for Good' Movement."

49. Svoboda, "Rise of the 'Gaming for Good' Movement." In addition
to shaping student behavior, the game provides teachers with readily
available data on each student: "Graves was impressed with how quickly
the game supplied him with a wealth of information on all 125 students'

social acumen. 'At the end of the day, I had data for my entire grade level and on each individual student,' he says. 'I was able to sit down with [the teachers] and explain what it revealed about social skills that kids were struggling with.'" Melissa DeRosier is the creator of *Zoo U.* See Melissa DeRosier et al., *"Zoo U: A Stealth Approach to Social Skills Assessment in Schools," Advances in Human-Computer Interaction* (2012): 1–7, http://www.hindawi.com/journals/ahci/2012/654791/.

50. "Games for Learning," 3C Institute, https://www.3cisd.com/learning-games.

51. DeRosier et al., *"Zoo U,"* 1.

52. Majia Nadesan demonstrates how "risk" is constructed differently across racialized and classed populations, where affluent students are at risk of anxiety and poor students are at risk of dropping out, pregnancy, or drug use. See Majia Holmer Nadesan, *Governing Childhood into the 21st Century: Biopolitical Technologies of Childhood Management and Education* (New York: Palgrave Macmillan, 2010).

53. Elizabeth Jones, "When Educational Games Work: Mission U.S. Demonstrates Best of Video Game Learning," PBS NewsHour, June 27, 2014, http://www.pbs.org/newshour/rundown/educational-games-work-mission-u-s-demonstrates-best-video-game-learning/.

54. See Nikolas Rose, "Governing the Enterprising Self," in *The Values of the Enterprise Culture: The Moral Debate,* ed. Paul Heelas and Paul Morris, 141–64 (New York: Routledge, 1992); and Laurie Ouellette and James Hay, *Better Living through Reality TV* (Malden, Mass.: Blackwell, 2008).

55. Specter, "In Support of 'Flight to Freedom.'"

56. Johnson, "On Agency," 116. Saidiya Hartman makes a similar argument in *Scenes of Subjection: Terror, Slavery, and Self-Making in Nineteenth-Century America* (New York: Oxford University Press, 1997).

57. Although Johnson is writing specifically about liberalism and liberal agency, I understand neoliberal subjectivity to be a heightened version of liberal subjectivity, placing more emphasis on becoming an enterprising, self-branding subject constituted through market logic.

58. Angela Davis, "Reflections on the Black Woman's Role in the Community of Slaves," in *The Angela Y. Davis Reader,* ed. Joy James (Malden, Mass.: Blackwell, 1998), 114.

59. Amber Jamilla Musser, *Sensational Flesh: Race, Power, and Masochism* (New York: NYU Press, 2014), 96.

60. Mission US, "Teacher's Guide: Content Briefing."

61. Specter, "In Support of 'Flight to Freedom.'"

62. The American Graduate website prominently features photographs of Black children and notes that "minority [students], English-language

learners, and students with disabilities" are particularly at risk and in need of "greater supports" in order to graduate high school. Additionally, American Graduate's "2016 Building a Grad Nation Report" includes appendices with graduation rates broken down by "race/ethnicity." "2016 Building a Grad Nation Report," Grad Nation, May 9, 2016, http://www.americangraduate.org/blogs/latest-education-headlines/2016/05/09/building-a-gradnation-2016-communities-states-have-work-to-do-to-reach-90/. Alexander Weheliye, *Habeas Viscus: Racializing Assemblages, Biopolitics, and Black Feminist Theories of the Human* (Durham, N.C.: Duke University Press, 2014), cited in Ralina Joseph, *Postracial Resistance: Black Women, Media, and the Uses of Strategic Ambiguity* (New York: NYU Press, 2018), 211.

63. Mission US, "Mission 2: 'Flight to Freedom' Educator Guide," https://assets.mission-us.org/wp-content/uploads/2019/12/26210532/complete_flight_to_freedom_classroom_guide_final.pdf.

64. Johnson, "On Agency," 113–14.

65. Johnson, 114.

66. Johnson, 114–15.

67. Johnson, 115.

68. Johnson, 115. Alexander Weheliye grapples with this question in *Habeas Viscus.*

69. Johnson, "On Agency," 121.

70. Stephanie Smallwood, "The Politics of the Archive and History's Accountability to the Enslaved," *History of the Present: A Journal of Critical History* 6, no. 2 (2016): 126–27.

71. See Lisa Nakamura, *Digitizing Race: Visual Cultures of the Internet* (Minneapolis: University of Minnesota Press, 2008); and Safiya Noble, *Algorithms of Oppression: How Search Engines Reinforce Racism* (New York: NYU Press, 2018).

72. See Virginia Eubanks, *Automating Inequality: How High-Tech Tools Profile, Police, and Punish the Poor* (New York: St. Martin's, 2017).

73. Kirk Hamilton, "They Made a Video Game about Slavery, and It's Actually Good," Kotaku, February 14, 2012, http://kotaku.com/5885194/they-made-a-video-game-about-slavery-and-its-actually-good.

74. Hamilton, "They Made a Video Game about Slavery."

75. Anable, "Casual Games." See also Alexander Galloway, "Social Realism in Gaming," *Game Studies: The International Journal of Computer Game Research* 4, no. 1 (2004): http://www.gamestudies.org/0401/galloway/.

76. Mission US, "Mission 2: 'Flight to Freedom' Educator Guide."

77. Musser, *Sensational Flesh,* 102.

78. Hamilton, "They Made a Video Game about Slavery."

79. Mission US, "Teacher's Guide: Learning Goals, Mission 2: 'Flight to Freedom,'" https://www.mission-us.org/teach/flight-to-freedom/teaching-this-mission/learning-goals/.

80. Musser, *Sensational Flesh*, 101.

81. Stacy Zeiger, "Mission US: Think Fast! About the Past," app review, Common Sense Education, December 2013, https://www.commonsense.org/education/app/mission-us-think-fast-about-the-past.

4. "How Many Slaves Work for You?"

1. Dan Mellamphy and Nandita Biswas Mellamphy, "An Algorithmic Agartha: Post-App Approaches to Synarchic Regulation," *Fibreculture Journal* 25 (2015): 169. See also Clemens Apprich, Wendy Hui Kyong Chun, Florian Cramer, and Hito Steyerl, *Pattern Discrimination* (Minneapolis: University of Minnesota Press, 2019). For more on the discourse of neutrality with respect to technology, see Stacy Wood, "Police Body Cameras: Emotional Mediation and the Economies of Visuality," *Emotions, Technology, and Design* (2016): 1–15.

2. See Virginia Eubanks, *Automating Inequality: How High-Tech Tools Profile, Police, and Punish the Poor* (New York: St. Martin's, 2017). For more on the relationship between race and algorithms, see Safiya Noble, *Algorithms of Oppression: How Search Engines Reinforce Racism* (New York: NYU Press, 2018).

3. Ephrat Livni, "In the US, Some Criminal Court Judges Now Use Algorithms to Guide Decisions on Bail," *Quartz*, February 28, 2017, https://qz.com/920196/criminal-court-judges-in-new-jersey-now-use-algorithms-to-guide-decisions-on-bail/.

4. Cathy O'Neil, *Weapons of Math Destruction: How Big Data Increases Inequality and Threatens Democracy* (New York: Crown, 2017), 164.

5. In "Wasting the Future," Sabine LeBel details the long-standing fetish of new technology and suggests that the future-oriented "technological sublime" discourse evinces a strong belief in "the promise of social harmony" through supposedly better technology and communication. LeBel, "Wasting the Future: The Technological Sublime, Communications Technologies, and E-waste," *Communication +1* 1, no. 1 (2012): 1–19, 9.

6. In a 2016 interview, founder Justin Dillon explains that the State Department approached Call + Response after the organization's 2008 documentary film was released. According to Dillon, the State Department "wanted to create a website where any consumer could find out how they are directly connected to the issue through the products that they own." Dillon underscores that the letters consumers wrote to companies

were written with "no anger, no vitriol." See Joshua New, "5 Q's for Justin Dillon, Founder of Made in a Free World," Center for Data Innovation, March 14, 2016, https://www.datainnovation.org/2016/03/5-qs-for-justin -dillon-founder-of-made-in-a-free-world/.

7. Slavery Footprint, https://slaveryfootprint.org/.

8. Paula Ioanide, *The Emotional Politics of Racism: How Feelings Trump Facts in an Era of Colorblindness* (Stanford, Calif.: Stanford University Press, 2015), 114.

9. Justin Dillon, "Breaking News: Sec. John Kerry introduces FRDM," fundraising email from Made in a Free World, June 20, 2014.

10. Peter Chow-White, "The Informationalization of Race: Communication Technologies and the Human Genome in the Digital Age," *International Journal of Communication* 2 (2008): 1168–94. For more on U.S. media culture's uptake of *postracial,* see Catherine Squires, *The Post-Racial Mystique: Media and Race in the Twenty-First Century* (New York: NYU Press, 2014); and Ralina Joseph, *Postracial Resistance: Black Women, Media, and the Uses of Strategic Ambiguity* (New York: NYU Press, 2018).

11. Lawrence Glickman dates U.S. consumer activism to the Revolutionary War era but notes that the nineteenth century laid the groundwork for modern consumer activism. Further, whereas consumers during the American Revolution were urged to "withhold their patronage from unsavory merchants who sold goods of British origins," during the nineteenth century, consuming "positively" emerged and consumers were urged to actualize "their ethical views through the consumption" of "ethical" goods. In this way, "one could consume rather than sacrifice to enact other ethical commitments." See Glickman, *Buying Power: A History of Consumer Activism in America* (Chicago: University of Chicago Press, 2009), 64.

12. FRDM, accessed January 19, 2021, https://frdm.co/.

13. Ariel Schwartz, "How Many Slaves Made Your Stuff? It's Now Easier for Companies to Discover the Truth," Fast Company, February 2, 2015, http://www.fastcoexist.com/3041009/change-generation/how-many -slaves-made-your-stuff-its-now-easier-for-companies-to-discover-t.

14. See Samantha King, *Breast Cancer and the Politics of Philanthropy* (Minneapolis: University of Minnesota Press, 2008); Jo Littler, *Radical Consumption: Shopping for Change in Contemporary Culture* (Maidenhead, U.K.: Open University Press, 2009); Tania Lewis and Emily Potter, eds., *Ethical Consumption: A Critical Introduction* (New York: Routledge, 2010); Roopali Mukherjee and Sarah Banet-Weiser, *Commodity Activism: Cultural Resistance in Neoliberal Times* (New York: NYU Press, 2012); and Sarah Banet-Weiser, *Authentic^{TM}: The Politics of Ambivalence in a Brand Culture* (New York: NYU Press, 2012).

15. Alison Hearn, "'Meat, Mask, Burden': Probing the Contours of the Branded 'Self,'" *Journal of Consumer Culture* 8, no. 2 (2008): 197–217.

16. Banet-Weiser, *Authentic^{TM}*, 127.

17. Banet-Weiser, 136.

18. Paula Chakravartty and Sreela Sarkar, "Entrepreneurial Justice: The New Spirit of Capitalism in Emergent India," *Popular Communication* 11 (2013): 59.

19. See, for example, C. K. Prahalad, *Fortune at the Bottom of the Pyramid: Eradicating Poverty through Profits* (Upper Saddle River, N.J.: Wharton School, 2010).

20. Justin Dillon, "This Is What Freedom Looks Like," fundraising email, October 30, 2015.

21. Jo Littler and Liz Moor, "Fourth Worlds and Neo-Fordism," *Cultural Studies* 22, no. 5 (2008): 720.

22. "About Us," If You Care, accessed February 22, 2021, https://www.ifyoucare.com/pages/about-us.

23. Rebecca Horne, "Tabulate Your 'Slavery Footprint,'" *Wall Street Journal,* November 11, 2011, http://blogs.wsj.com/ideas-market/2011/11/22/tabulate-your-slavery-footprint/.

24. Robin DiAngelo, *White Fragility: Why It's So Hard for White People to Talk about Racism* (Boston: Beacon, 2018), 2.

25. Slavery Footprint, accessed March 26, 2018, https://slaveryfootprint.org/.

26. DiAngelo, *White Fragility*.

27. Andrew Martin, "Slavery Becomes a Personal Question Online," *New York Times,* September 21, 2011.

28. Slavery Footprint, accessed March 26, 2018, https://slaveryfootprint.org/.

29. Glickman, "'Buy for the Sake of the Slave,'" 893.

30. Glickman, 895–96.

31. Glickman, 899.

32. The Slavery Footprint website was the topic of a graphic design blog that marveled at the effectiveness of its clean aesthetic: "Simple icons and childlike colors respond to your touch, moving to and fro, in and out, teaching you about modern slavery and calculating your 'footprint.'" When a commenter on the post raised the issue of emotion and how the site's design "insulates [him] to a certain extent from anger" given its emotional disconnect from the content, the original poster responded, "Slavery is egregious, but my sense is that the remedy begins with engagement, not anger. You basically have an invisible problem—slaves in the supply chain—that needs to be made visible, which the site does beautifully,

without accusation. So no defenses go up. Once visible, action can be taken." John McWade, "How Many Slaves Work for You?" *Before & After's Design Talk* (blog), April 18, 2012, http://www.mcwade.com/DesignTalk/2012/04/the-money-is-in-the-story/; Mushtaq Farooqui, April 19, 2012, comment on McWade; and John McWade, April 19, 2012, reply to Mushtaq Farooqui.

33. Glickman, "'Buy for the Sake of the Slave,'" 898.

34. Thank you to Sarah Banet-Weiser for alerting me to this observation.

35. "FRDM Video," Made in a Free World, accessed March 26, 2018, http://www.madeinafreeworld.com/business/?utm_source=email1&utm_medium=email&utm_campaign=Kerry%20announcement#FRDMvideo, accessed March 26, 2018.

36. "FRDM Video."

37. Justin Dillon, "Breaking News: Sec. John Kerry introduces FRDM," fundraising email from Made in a Free World, June 20, 2014.

38. Stephan Magura, "Ariba and Made in a Free World Mitigate Slavery in the Supply Chain," SAP Press Release, July 23, 2015, http://news.sap.com/ariba-made-in-a-free-world-mitigating-slavery-in-the-supply-chain/. For an analysis of the entanglement between race and algorithmic culture, see Lisa Nakamura, *Digitizing Race: Visual Cultures of the Internet* (Minneapolis: University of Minnesota Press, 2008); Apprich, Chun, Cramer, and Steyerl, *Pattern Discrimination*; Tara McPherson, "U.S. Operating Systems at Midcentury: The Intertwining of Race and Unix," in *The Visual Culture Reader*, 3rd ed., ed. Nicholas Mirzoeff, 591–604 (New York: Routledge, 2013).

39. Justin Dillon, "Did You Feel That?" email from Made in a Free World, April 10, 2015.

40. O'Neil, *Weapons of Math Destruction*, 216–17.

41. Allison Page, "It's Easy to Be Green," *In Media Res,* June 4, 2013, http://mediacommons.org/imr/2013/04/15/its-easy-being-green.

42. Julie Guthman, "'If They Only Knew': Color Blindness and Universalism in California Alternative Food Institutions," *Professional Geographer* 60, no. 3 (2008): 388.

43. Guthman, "'If They Only Knew,'" 391.

44. Glickman, "'Buy for the Sake of the Slave,'" 903.

45. Glickman, 904.

46. Slavery Footprint, accessed February 2, 2018, https://slaveryfootprint.org/.

47. Slavery Footprint, accessed March 26, 2018, https://slaveryfootprint.org/.

48. Saidiya Hartman, *Lose Your Mother: A Journey along the Atlantic*

Slave Route (New York: Farrar, Straus and Giroux, 2007), 6. See also Christina Sharpe, *Monstrous Intimacies: Making Post-Slavery Subjects* (Durham, N.C.: Duke University Press, 2010). The site does not consider U.S. prison labor to be forced labor.

49. Tryon Woods, "Surrogate Selves: Notes on Anti-trafficking and Anti-blackness," *Social Identities* 19, no. 1 (2013): 120.

50. Woods, "Surrogate Selves," 130.

51. Made in a Free World, https://madeinafreeworld.org/. This is an oft-repeated phrase for the antitrafficking movement. See, for example, Terrence McNally, "There Are More Slaves Today Than at Any Time in Human History," *Alternet*, January 12, 2015, https://www.alternet.org/2015/01/there-are-more-slaves-today-any-time-human-history/.

52. Kevin Bales, *Disposable People: New Slavery in the Global Economy* (Berkeley: University of California Press, 1999), 9.

53. Woods, "Surrogate Selves," 129.

54. Olivia Lewis, "Conner Prairie Slavery Re-enactment Draws Criticism," *IndyStar*, August 6, 2016, https://www.indystar.com/story/news/2016/08/06/conner-prairie-slavery-re-enactment-draws-criticism/82987036/.

55. During the panel "What Does It Mean to Play a Slave? The 'Follow the North Star' Experiment" at the American Studies Association Annual Meeting on October 10, 2015, panelists described their experiences with the Follow the North Star program, noting the announcement about Slavery Footprint at the conclusion of the program. https://asa.press.jhu.edu/program15/saturday.html.

56. Apologists for sweatshop labor argue that sweatshops are the better option given the alternatives. See Nicholas Kristof, "My Sweatshop Column," *New York Times*, January 14, 2009, http://kristof.blogs.nytimes.com/2009/01/14/my-sweatshop-column/.

57. Saidiya Hartman, *Scenes of Subjection: Terror, Slavery, and Self-Making in Nineteenth-Century America* (New York: Oxford University Press, 1997).

58. Hartman, *Scenes of Subjection*, 116. Marx offers a similar critique of the tenets of the Enlightenment and liberal democracy in the *Grundrisse*: "The sphere of circulation or commodity exchange, within whose boundaries the sale and purchase of labour-power goes on, is in fact a very Eden of the innate rights of man. It is the exclusive realm of Freedom, Equality, Property and Bentham." See Karl Marx, *Grundrisse*, trans. Martin Nicolaus (London: Penguin Books, 1993), 280.

59. "Methodology," Slavery Footprint, accessed June 21, 2014, http://slaveryfootprint.org/about/#methodology.

60. Seth Rockman, "The Unfree Origins of American Capitalism," in *The Economy of Early America: Historical Perspectives and New Directions*, ed. Cathy D. Matson, 335–61 (University Park: Pennsylvania State University Press, 2006).

61. David Roediger, *The Wages of Whiteness: Race and the Making of the American Working Class* (New York: Verso, 2007).

62. Rockman, "Unfree Origins of American Capitalism," 350–51.

63. Barack Obama, "Remarks by the President to the Clinton Global Initiative," White House Office of the Press Secretary, September 25, 2012, http://www.whitehouse.gov/the-press-office/2012/09/25/remarks-president-clinton-global-initiative.

Conclusion

1. Kara Walker, *Kara Walker: My Complement, My Enemy, My Oppressor, My Love*, Walker Art Center, Minneapolis, Minn., February 17–May 13, 2007, https://walkerart.org/calendar/2007/kara-walker-my-complement-my-enemy-my-oppress.

2. Target's headquarters is based in Minneapolis and the company is a corporate sponsor of the Walker Art Center, funding the museum's First Fridays.

3. There were several news stories focused on people's responses (and their offensiveness). See Alison Herman, "Kara Walker Knew People Would Take Dumb Selfies with 'A Subtlety,' and That Shouldn't Surprise Us," *FlavorWire*, October 14, 2014, https://www.flavorwire.com/482585/kara-walker-knew-people-would-take-dumb-selfies-with-a-subtlety-and-that-shouldnt-surprise-us; and Alyssa Rosenberg, "Selfie Culture and Kara Walker's 'A Subtlety,'" *Washington Post*, June 30, 2014, https://www.washingtonpost.com/news/act-four/wp/2014/06/30/selfie-culture-and-kara-walkers-a-subtlety/.

4. Maryemma Graham, *Conversations with Margaret Walker* (Jackson: University Press of Mississippi, 2002), 133.

5. Robert Nemiroff to Grant A. Tinker, Chairman of the Board of NBC, April 5, 1982, box 43, folder 10, Schomburg Center for Research in Black Culture, New York.

6. Marie Torre, *New York Herald Tribune*, August 30, 1960, box 43, folder 14, Lorraine Hansberry Collection, Schomburg Center for Research in Black Culture, New York.

7. Robert Nemiroff to Grant Tinker, April 5, 1982, box 43, folder 10, Lorraine Hansberry Collection, Schomburg Center for Research in Black Culture, New York.

8. For a rich analysis of how Black women writers and visual artists engage with slavery's afterlife, see Kimberly Juanita Brown, *The Repeating Body: Slavery's Visual Resonance in the Contemporary* (Durham, N.C.: Duke University Press, 2015).

9. James Baldwin, *Nobody Knows My Name: More Notes of a Native Son* (New York: Dial, 1961).

10. Roderick Ferguson, "Sissies at the Picnic: The Subjugated Knowledges of a Black Rural Queer," in *Feminist Waves, Feminist Generations: Life Stories from the Academy,* ed. Hokulani Aikau, Karla Erickson, and Jennifer Pierce, 188–96 (Minneapolis: University of Minnesota Press, 2007), 194.

11. Kara Walker, *An Audience,* wall didactic, Domino Sugar Factory, Brooklyn, N.Y., 2014, courtesy of Sikkema Jenkins.

12. Glenda Carpio, "On the Whiteness of Kara Walker's *Marvelous Sugar Baby,*" *ASAP/Journal* 2, no. 3 (2017): 552.

13. Carpio, "On the Whiteness," 552.

14. Carpio, 556. Creative Time, the organization that commissioned the exhibition, actively invited visitors to contribute to the *Digital Sugar Baby.*

15. Carpio, 558.

16. Carpio, 566.

17. Walker, *An Audience.*

18. For more on privacy and "the right to die" with respect to Blackness and digital space, see Tonia Sutherland, "Making a Killing: On Race, Ritual, and (Re)Membering in Digital Culture," *Preservation, Digital Technology & Culture* 46, no. 1 (2017): 32–40.

19. Walker, *An Audience.*

20. Herman, "Kara Walker Knew People Would Take Dumb Selfies."

21. See Stephanie Smallwood, "The Politics of the Archive and History's Accountability to the Enslaved," *History of the Present: A Journal of Critical History* 6, no. 2 (2016): 129.

22. Carpio, "On the Whiteness," 561.

23. Walker, *An Audience.*

24. Carpio, "On the Whiteness," 568, 563.

25. Hartman, *Scenes of Subjection,* 18–19.

26. Carpio, "On the Whiteness," 561.

27. Amanda Hess, "Earning the 'Woke' Badge," *New York Times,* April 19, 2016, https://www.nytimes.com/2016/04/24/magazine/earning-the-woke-badge.html.

Index

ABC (network): Department of Broadcast Standards and Practices, 74–75, 76; documentaries, 26; *Roots* and, 53, 58, 60, 73, 76, 108

"Abolitioning" (web series episode), 2

abolitionists, 2–3, 99–100, 114, 120

activism: antiracist, 4, 6, 59; antiwar, 150n63; Black, 24, 35, 37–39, 41, 55; civil rights, 9, 11, 14, 19, 21, 24, 59, 95; consumer, 17, 105–12, 120, 168n11; free produce, 111, 115; global, 23

admiration, white, 6, 49–50, 59, 61, 81, 101

affect, 6, 8, 12–13, 27, 71, 74–75, 85, 97, 108, 130, 143–44n8. *See also* emotion

affective governance: about, 3–7, 10–11, 79, 125; data and, 104; documentary format and, 25; edugames and, 88–89, 92; *Roots* and, 54

Africa, 56, 59

African Americans: history of, 81, 94; incorporation into the nation, 50; portrayed in *Flight to Freedom*, 80–81, 159n6; struggles of, 6, 28–29, 49–50, 59, 61, 81, 101. *See also* Black people

afterlife of slavery: Black women artists and, 173n8; documentaries and, 29, 36–38; *Flight to Freedom* and, 80; *Roots* and, 62–63, 70, 78; Slavery Footprint and, 17, 105, 116–17; visual and, 5–9; whiteness and, 134

agency, Black, 16, 80–81, 86–87, 92–96, 99, 101–2, 160n9, 165n57

Ahmed, Sara, 6, 69

algorithmic culture, 105, 111, 170n38

algorithmic governance, 17, 103–4, 108, 114, 120, 125

algorithms: FRDM and, 112–13, 117; race and, 96, 103, 117, 120–21, 167n2, 170n38; to uncover forced labor, 113, 120; video games and, 84, 97, 162–63n41

alternative food movements, 114

American Apparel (brand), 107

American History and Civics Initiative, 83

American Psychological Association, 90

American Psychologist (journal), 90

American Social History Project, 80

America's Army (video game), 88

Anable, Aubrey, 82, 97

anger, Black: documentaries and, 14–15, 20, 24, 25, 30–37, 41, 45–46, 48; emotional

management of, 79, 90, 149n52;
Roots and, 50, 51, 125
Antebellum (film), 4
antebellum era, 11
antiracism: formal, 23–24; liberal,
55, 62; official, 4–6, 8–11, 15,
20–22, 26–27, 31–32, 44, 47–49,
68, 73, 81; performative, 101, 121,
131, 133; whiteness and, 11, 21, 24,
26, 47, 72, 125
antitrafficking movement, 116, 117
apartheid, legalized, 21
Ask a Slave (web series), 1–3, 9
Assassin's Creed (video game), 7
Audience, An (video), 17, 124, 125,
127–35

bail, cash, 103
Baldwin, James, 125
Bales, Kevin, 117
Bambara, Toni Cade, 17, 125
Banet-Weiser, Sarah, 106
Bell & Howell Close-Up! series, 20,
26, 33
Benton, Charles, 52
Berlin Wall, 62
Best, Stephen, 40
Bicentennial, U.S., 48, 50, 60–61,
154n45
Birth of a Nation, The (film), 4
Black. White (TV program), 85
Black History Month, 79
Black Like Me (Griffin), 85
Black Lives Matter, 78, 134
Black Muslims, 34, 35
Blackness: anti-, 11, 23, 63, 116;
criminality and, 150n68; digital
space and, 173n18; documen-
taries and, 11, 20–21, 23, 24, 28,
33–35, 37–38, 42, 44–45, 126;

Flight to Freedom and, 16, 82,
92; *Roots* and, 47, 69; slavery's
afterlife and, 5; Walker's works
and, 125, 127, 132; white people
embodying, 85; whiteness produced through, 2–3, 20, 146n2
Black people: Black nationalism,
20, 30, 34, 35, 36, 42; children,
128–30, 165–66n62; feminism,
3, 9, 10, 17–18, 64–67, 75–76,
125–27, 132–33; matriarchs, 22,
63–64; pathology of, 8, 21, 22,
33–34, 45, 64; students, 56, 87,
117; suffering of, 45, 63, 69, 116;
violence by, 38, 40–42, 131;
women, 64–65, 74–76, 148n21,
148n25. *See also* African Americans; anger, Black; pride, Black
Black Power movement, 8, 11, 13,
21, 36–37, 39–40, 45, 48, 54–55,
149n52
"Black Power, White Backlash"
(documentary episode), 20, 24,
38–43
Black Rage (Grier and Cobbs), 34,
149n52
Bluem, A. William, 21, 25
Bodroghkozy, Aniko, 43
Bogost, Ian, 88
bonded labor, 109–10
brand culture, 106, 112, 114, 115, 116,
118
Bromberg, Walter, 34–35
Brown, Kimberly Juanita, 5
Burke, Edmund, 43
Burton, LeVar, 77, 78

Cacho, Lisa Marie, 8
Call + Response (nonprofit), 104,
167n6

Allison Page is assistant professor of media studies with a joint appointment in the Institute for the Humanities and the Department of Communication and Theatre Arts at Old Dominion University.